Teaching Music
with Promise

Conducting, Rehearsing and Inspiring

PETER LOEL BOONSHAFT

Published by
MEREDITH MUSIC PUBLICATIONS
a division of G.W. Music, Inc.
4899 Lerch Creek Ct., Galesville, MD 20765
http://www.meredithmusic.com

MEREDITH MUSIC PUBLICATIONS and its stylized double M logo
are trademarks of
MEREDITH MUSIC PUBLICATIONS, a division of G.W. Music, Inc.

International Standard Book Number: 978-1-57463-112-8
Cataloging-in-Publication Data is on file with the Library of Congress.
Library of Congress Control Number: 2009929875
Printed and bound in U.S.A

DEDICATION

For my wife, Martha, and my children, Meredith Ann, Peter Loel and Matthew Christopher who have been and always will be my constant source of joy, wonder and beauty in the world. Thank you for your patience and encouragement, your laughter and tears, your spirit and encouragement. I will never be able to express how much you mean to me but I can tell you how much I love you, always.

ACKNOWLEDGEMENTS

To Dr. Garwood Whaley, Bruce Bush, Reber Clark and Nancy Bittner, thank you for the endlessness of your support, depth of your wisdom and abundance of your kindness. Know that how much I appreciate your help is second only to how much I cherish our friendship.

To Dr. Lynn Brinckmeyer, thank you for writing the foreword to this book, but much more important, thank you for the joy, talent and vision you bring to music education through your infectious enthusiasm and vibrant spirit. Thank you, my dear friend for simply being who you are.

To my family, friends and colleagues, thank you for your encouragement and inspiration.

And, most important, thank you to all of my students who have allowed me the privilege and honor of learning from them. I hope you know how much I appreciate and cherish each of you.

CONTENTS

FOREWORD

Who would have thought it possible for Peter Boon-shaft to top *Teaching Music with Passion* and *Teaching Music with Purpose*? But he certainly has, and I thank him for reminding us to energize our approach to life and teaching every day. As are his two previous books, this one is filled with stories and peppered with practical, hands-on information that will produce immediate results.

I am certain that *Teaching Music with Promise* will serve as a resource for all of us. He skillfully breaks down complex ideas into digestible pieces. This book is accessible, but don't let that fool you, because when Peter writes about the challenges of teaching difficult concepts, he also keeps us thinking about connections we make with others, while encouraging us to be the most musical conductors and musicians possible.

Although he offers pragmatic teaching strategies that can be used the very next day, his most valuable messages and lessons focus on nurturing the humanity of the people we teach. Peter's stories bring life and relevancy to the points he makes throughout the book. He offers up a mix of realistic suggestions interspersed with philosophical reflections and anecdotes that will touch your soul.

Anyone who keeps up with such things knows that Peter's name is listed on conference programs all across the country as a speaker, clinician and conductor. People flock to his sessions, irrespective of what area of music education they teach, because he reminds us of *how* we should teach and *why* we teach music. His uncanny ability to connect information and relate it to our world persuades us to hold ourselves accountable, and to consistently strive for excellence.

One of the most inviting characteristics about Peter is that he is an educator first, and he eagerly shares the vast knowledge he has acquired through his journey of teaching, conducting and performing music. Those who have seen him conduct or teach know that he backs up every recommendation in his books by practicing them consistently. When we watch him lead a band or orchestra we almost feel like an intruder eavesdropping on an intimate conversation between him and the instrumentalists under his direction. Even though the artistry is important, it never takes precedence over the people who are playing in his ensembles or sitting in his classes. Peter is a true friend to music education. His writing exemplifies that, as he personifies the human being we wish to be.

Dr. Lynn Brinckmeyer
Director of Choral Music Education, Texas State University
Past President, MENC: The National Association for Music Education

PREFACE:
PROMISES MADE

It had been one of those weeks. Thanks to some very poor planning on my part I had crossed the country from coast to coast six times in eight days, including two red-eye flights through the night. Don't ask why. Let's just say that my brain still thinks I'm twenty-five though my body knows the truth of the matter. If that wasn't bad enough, severe winter weather caused delay upon delay upon delay. After over a week of this I arrived home in New York late one evening run ragged, left with raw nerves, little patience, a faint memory of what sleep felt like and the desire to curl up in a corner somewhere and hide from the world. But I couldn't.

That's right, you guessed it: the next morning I had to be at the airport by 4:45 for yet another flight to another state on the West Coast. So after unpacking and repacking my suitcase, an extravagant four hours of sleep and a leisurely breakfast of black coffee on the run, I was off to catch my flight. It was pitch black outside, well below freezing, with snow everywhere. Walking down the driveway from my house I slipped and fell on the ice. Now wet, cold and sore,

I drove to the airport, seething. I was at wit's end, dreading a day that had barely started.

I boarded the airplane and just sat there as waves of feeling frazzled, hungry, exhausted, drained and angry surged through me. I was anything but hopeful, everything but positive. The darkness outside was a perfect match for my mood. Well, as we taxied away from the ramp, I started doing paperwork so I could add some worry about how far behind I was to my gloominess. As we flew south to avoid yet another storm, something caught my eye outside the window.

It was a tiny glimmer of light. It almost looked like a spark way off in the distance and as I continued to stare at it the little shard of brightness grew larger and larger filling the darkness with radiance. I couldn't take my eyes off it. It was captivating. It was mesmerizing. It was overwhelming. It was magnificent. It was a sunrise. Now I've watched sunrises before, glancing occasionally at that beautiful sight, but this was different. On that day I didn't just watch a *sunrise*, I watched the *sun rise*. I watched as it filled emptiness with brilliance and shattered uncertainty with clarity. Its luster brought optimism. Its glow signaled hope. It was the light of promise.

As I watched, all the ills I carried with me onto that airplane slipped away, my spirit uplifted, my mood transformed. I was charged with excitement about the trip I had dreaded little more than an hour before. My thoughts filled with the possibilities of what was ahead of me, the enjoyment around the corner and the importance of every moment I get to make music with young people. I smiled with enthusiasm as that light revealed what really mattered. With that sunrise I realized what I guess I always knew — what each of us always knew — that along with teaching music with passion and teaching music with purpose, it is our teaching music with promise that may make all the difference in the lives of our students.

The promise of teaching found in every new day, in what the future holds, in the untapped potential we help every child realize. The promise we affirm as teachers to make a difference, to help students discover the person they are and the person they can become. The promise of knowledge, skills, creativity and caring. The promise of hope, enthusiasm, optimism and resolve. The promise of high expectations, profound dedication, unending commitment, sincere concern and heartfelt counsel. Quite simply, the promise of a teacher.

Teacher, instructor, mentor — by whatever name you call them — those who have devoted themselves to bettering the world one person at a time. Those who excite minds, deepen hearts, touch souls and change lives. Those whose impact is greater than any moment in time, whose reach is farther than any place, whose destiny is more profound than any estimation, whose promise is more valuable than any fortune.

May you realize your gifts and cherish your importance. May you seek out and find those everyday moments of joy and happiness. May you cherish every smile, every tear and every laugh. May you reflect upon all you do for your students, that which may be found on a staff of music and that which is so much greater.

I hope the pages that follow help remind you of just those things, for that is why they were written. I wish they were filled with wisdom and answers. They are not.

Honestly, the older I get the more I realize the sad truth that *the more I know, the more I know I don't know*. So I have no answers, no truths, no "right way" of doing anything. We find those for ourselves on our journey as teachers.

For the *answers* we seek depend on the questions we pose, the *truths* we hold dear come from our willingness to search for new ideas, and the *path* we ultimately embrace comes from our challenging every belief as we constantly strive to find our own *best way*. This book is simply a collection of thoughts for us to share and ideas to ponder as we do just that, humbly offered in the spirit of the wonderful old saying: "The fool is proud he knows so much, the wise man ashamed he knows no more."

Much of what follows are ideas my teachers — and even more often my students — helped me learn. It is my hope they know how much they have meant and will always mean to me. They are part of me and will always serve to motivate me to become the teacher I someday hope to be.

These pages also include many quotes from others whose words are far greater than mine. Know that every effort was made to correctly attribute those thoughts; however, where the author is believed to be unknown, no ascription was made.

I also want to thank each of you for reading these pages and sharing this journey with me. The depth of my gratitude is only surpassed by my appreciation for all you do, for your dedication to your students and the joy you share with all those whom you touch through music.

With each new day, each new sunrise, we have the opportunity to imagine what can be and make it happen. For each of us the excitement of every new beginning is the promise of what lies ahead, what can be, what the future holds. Much like an artist looks at a blank canvas and sees the beauty that will soon be created, we as teachers see the child that can be, a treasure waiting to be discovered, ever mindful that what we *see* depends on what we *look* for. Never lose sight of that incredible responsibility or the richness of that calling.

But maybe when all is said and done, the best way to really describe teaching is to borrow a sentiment from the inimitable Marx Brothers, with the query: Did you know that there is a million bucks hidden in the house next door? The reply: But there is no house next door. Undaunted, the response: No? Then let's go build one.

Funny as it may be, isn't that just what you do every day? You see the fortune all children are as you build the house they will find themselves in. And that, my friends, is the promise of teaching. ▨

The Things
That Matter

I have always felt that one of the most important aspects of working with young people is helping them to discover and express their emotions. It has meant more to me than any other facet of being a music teacher. Though we all do this in our own way it surely must be one of the great benefits of music education. To that end I try my best to show how music makes me feel as I conduct, hoping my example may help those more reticent students explore their feelings. And it is always a joy to watch their faces as they reveal those emotions.

However, nothing that important comes without risk. The risk we take is that those students who are uncomfortable with those emotions may express their discomfort with nervous giggles. It's human nature: people often laugh when ill at ease. But if we are committed to the goal of helping students to express themselves through music we must be willing to take that risk. The truth be known, I find that as long as students know our emotions are sincere, the giggles are rare indeed. Though one such time a student really got the better of me.

I was conducting a large honors band of delightful high school students. They were extremely talented and very focused but extraordinarily reserved. I don't just mean polite and quiet, I mean seemingly unmoved by the music they were making; their faces revealing little, their playing much the same. So I worked at getting them to *feel* as much as *think*, to express emotion as much as demonstrate facility. I tried my best to show them what I was feeling with hopes they would do the same through their music. Slowly, almost one by one, they started to blossom. It was wonderful: ninety young people playing from the heart. However, the more emotion I showed, the more one young oboist made her discomfort apparent with overt giggles. I just couldn't reach her; I was sure she just didn't get it.

This went on, more or less, throughout the first day of rehearsing. By the middle of the second day she wasn't giggling, but seemed unmoved by all around her. I was convinced I had failed to get through to her. Maybe she just wasn't willing to share her feelings. I decided I would have to accept the fact that outward expressions of emotion just weren't part of this young lady's personality.

By the third day, the day of the concert, the students were "playing the spots off the page." They were technically and musically playing at a level beyond their years. There wasn't a single moment in the entire program I was worried about — except one. It was a very exposed English horn solo at the start of a slow and somber work. The young boy playing the part tried diligently, but it demanded extremely soft and sustained playing, ending with a very long tone on the lowest note of the instrument.

Each time we rehearsed the passage it was basically a "coin toss" as to whether that last note, let alone a few of the

others, would speak. By concert time I think we all feared
the worst for this solo but hoped for the best. Though I was
willing to have another instrument play the part as cued by
the composer, the young man would have none of it. He was
determined to play every note, and I mean every note, of the
solo. We all knew the risk that came with that decision, but
we also knew in our hearts that he had earned the right to try.

Well, the evening concert was upon us. The students
took their seats on stage, the young man playing the English horn solo seated right next to the seemingly aloof oboist. The concert began. The ensemble played the first five
pieces of the performance with exceptional precision and
with remarkable expression. I could not have been prouder
of them — or so I thought. But now the moment I feared
was at hand. It was time for the work we all had a certain
amount of trepidation about. Before starting the piece, I
gave the young man playing the worrisome English horn
solo a smile with the most confident look I could muster,
though I must say the look he returned was a bit less com-
forting. Nonetheless, we started.

The first note of his solo spoke with determined clarity.
The joy we all felt was amazing but we also knew the biggest hurdle was still ahead. And as that last note sounded
with the subtlety and dignity of the most seasoned professional musician, we all beamed with delight. He had done
it. The entire ensemble, and its conductor, breathed a giant
sigh of relief coupled with a surge of intense exhilaration.
The powerful emotions we all felt were palpable. As the
work continued I looked him in the eyes, nodded and
smiled from ear to ear. He smiled back with a grin that was
as full of pride as it was relief.

A few seconds later, I guess just wanting to make sure he hadn't passed out, I glanced back over at him. And just when I thought nothing could make that moment more special, I watched as the oboist I feared I couldn't reach, with a tear running down her cheek, took her hand and patted the knee of that young man with all the sincerity, compassion and sensitivity you could imagine. Like a big sister wanting to show her little brother he had "done good," she looked him in the eyes and spoke from the heart without saying a word. How lucky I was to witness that sight, for it was one of the most touching, extraordinarily emotional displays I have ever seen.

It's amazing how gifts come to us in different packages and how people express emotions in many different ways. I guess we just have to do our best to help students express themselves in whatever way they choose, whenever they can, however they are comfortable. We've all been there, wondering whether we got through to a student. During those few days I thought I had lost that young lady; I hadn't. I just didn't know where to look. I thought she "just didn't get it"; she had. She knew what really mattered.

I'm so glad I caught that scene out of the corner of my eye for my life is richer for having done so. The emotional power of what we do, and the capacity of our students to bring it to life, have never ceased to amaze me, and probably never will. ▪

AND THERE SAT
FRANKLIN

I grew up in a wonderful community just outside of Phila-
delphia. Our home was filled with a great deal of love,
thanks in no small measure to a very large dog and three
cats. The veterinarian who cared for our four-legged family
members was a remarkably warm-hearted doctor known
for being a great veterinarian. He was also renowned for
having toilet-trained his own family's cats. That's right, you
read correctly, toilet-trained his cats. And having grown up
my whole childhood hearing about his (or was it his cats')
remarkable feat, I always wanted to have a toilet-trained
cat myself.

Now I told you that story so I could tell you this story.
Many, many years later when I was living in my first apartment, I got a cat; his name was Franklin. One weekend my
parents came to visit for a few days. After showing them
around the apartment, my dad and I sat down in the living
room to chat while my mom excused herself to go to the bathroom. The next thing I heard was my mom shrieking at the
top of her lungs in exasperated bafflement and quasi-disgust

as she walked in on Franklin as he was, well, let's just say using the toilet. That's right, Franklin my toilet-trained cat.

I ran to the bathroom and there was Mom pointing at the cat while he was doing his business. He looked at her as if to say, "Hey lady, can I have a little privacy here?" To say the least, Mom was shocked. To me it was normal. I was used to seeing my furry friend sitting on the toilet reading a good book (okay, I made the book part up). I became dulled to how odd it was. It became usual and normal to me.

Now I told you that story so I could tell you this story. A few years back I was invited to conduct in a town that was several hours' drive from the closest airport. After landing there I met my host, we jumped into his car and started our journey. Midway through our drive I began to smell something odd. Odd then grew to bad, bad grew to disgusting, disgusting grew to nauseating and nauseating grew to repulsive. Finally, in amazement at this stench, I asked my host what I was smelling. Completely unaffected, he nonchalantly replied, "Oh, that's the local paper mill."

I don't know if you've ever been near a paper mill, but let me tell you, they emit an odor that would offend a gaggle (okay, it's really a "wake") of buzzards feasting at the city garbage dump. It is a smell like no other. So there I was, gasping for breath, my eyes watering, my throat tightening, while he sat totally oblivious to the hideous stench. Then he said, "I guess when you're around it as much as I am, you don't even smell it anymore." How true. How incredibly true. He grew comfortable with something even as unpleasant as that smell. It simply became normal to him.

Now I told you that story so I could tell you this story. Last evening I attended a high school band concert. As the students walked onto the stage they looked polished and professional. Their posture was wonderful and they glowed with confidence. All of us in the audience were convinced a fabulous performance was in store. The conductor then began the first piece on the program and I'm guessing the band probably played reasonably well. Why am I guessing at how well they played, when I was sitting right in front of them, you ask? Because it was almost impossible to hear anything other than the bass drum being played at a volume that could only be described as mind-numbingly loud. I'm telling you sparks were coming off that bass drum beater.

From the first downbeat right through to the final stinger, I was convinced the bass drummer's part said, "Play so loudly that the ears of every member of the audience bleed." It was utterly astounding. I watched and listened in disbelief as the young man playing the bass drum beat the daylights out of the instrument with unbridled power. How could that have happened? How could the conductor's senses have become so dulled to that sound? How could he not have noticed it? Easily, if we are not careful and vigilant. We become used to it.

So why did I tell you that story? To remind us that we are all susceptible to things becoming *usual* enough that we expect them, accept them and grow oblivious to them. In the end maybe they won't be as obnoxious as that thunderous bass drum sound, but if they *creep into* our perception of normal, they can easily become ignored.

Let's imagine the first rehearsal of that band playing that piece. I can just picture the tempo turning a bit unstable as they sight-read the work and the conductor asking the bass drummer — who at that point was probably playing at a

modest volume—for a bit more. "A bit more" helped steady
the tempo and that dynamic level became usual. At subse-
quent rehearsals, the bass drummer now more confident,
"a bit more" turned into overly aggressive. Aggressive then
became normal. Over time, the bass drummer now brim-
ming with enthusiasm, aggressive grew to be obnoxious.
Unchecked and unaware, obnoxious simply became normal.

Over the course of months unnoticed, gradual increases
in that performer's volume could morph relatively easily
into musical disaster. Now does this excuse the terrible
performance I heard? No, but it can explain how our perception—if changed gradually enough or for long enough
periods of time—can be altered without our being aware of
it, allowing us to become used to just about anything. How
else could that conductor have become oblivious to his bass
drummer's playing, my host become unaware of the paper
mill's repulsive odor, or I grow so used to seeing my cat on a
toilet as to be unfazed?

Though that performance was unquestionably an
extreme example, and I am sure we would have caught
something as egregious as that bass drummer's performance
early on, it does remind us to be ever vigilant, ultra prepared,
keenly aware, highly focused and intensely observant. We
are all susceptible to that same kind of numbing of our senses
if we don't guard against it and take steps to prevent it.

We all need to step back from the situation to look and
listen for things that have become normal to us. True, most
of them won't be as thunderously blaring as a rampant
bass drummer, but they can be distracting or damaging
nonetheless. We know simply recording our rehearsals or
having our ensembles continue to play as we walk around

the rehearsal room or walk out into the auditorium can be amazingly insightful. Enlist the help of other music teachers in your school and district, local college instructors and retired music educators to listen to live or recorded rehearsals of your ensembles, giving you fresh sets of eyes and ears of those who can objectively critique the performance without the unconscious unawareness of that to which you have grown accustomed.

Changing our ensemble's setup or having the ensemble sit in random, scattered seating can offer us a different vantage point and perspective with just enough difference to shake up our perception of normal. Regularly attending professional performances and listening to recordings can also help keep us stay more focused and aware, refreshing our ears and minds as well as our ability to listen critically.

Quite simply, to fend off the problem of getting used to things in rehearsals, mix equal parts awareness, concern, concentration, observation and attentiveness. Stir in a fair amount of objectivity and serve it in the clear glass of keen perception, with a sprig of utter delight.

Like seeing something as unusual as a cat using the toilet, or smelling an odor offensive enough to curl hair, or hearing a student beating the daylights out of a bass drum, if we see, smell or hear anything often enough, unless we guard against it, it can become normal to us, rendering us completely and absolutely oblivious to it.

By the way, in case you ever come visit my home, let me warn you about our cat Janet, the one who knows how to turn on the water spigot when she wants a drink. But that's a story for another day. ▣

THREE LITTLE WORDS

"In a completely rational society," Lee Iacocca wrote, "the best of us would aspire to be teachers and the rest of us would have to settle for something less, because passing civilization along from one generation to the next generation ought to be the highest honor and the highest responsibility anyone could have."

I know Mr. Iacocca meant well with this statement, and I may be arguing semantics, but I strongly disagree with two points. First, the best of us *do* aspire to be teachers, and second, passing civilization along from one generation to the next generation *is* the highest honor and the highest responsibility anyone could have. For what could be more important? What could be of greater consequence?

In fact as teachers we are bound by three little words which encapsulate and crystallize the profound responsibility of our profession. Just as physicians pledge to bring honor to their profession with the promise of three little words, "primum non nocere," better known to most of us as "first, do no harm," we too are compelled by as solemn an obligation with three little words which are as humbling as they are empowering, as awesome as they are daunting.

It is said that with great honor comes great responsibility, and with the honor of being a teacher comes the responsibility of three little words in the Latin phrase, "in loco parentis," or "in the place of the parent." What could be more weighty a pledge than to promise to act in the best interest of every student? What could be more important an obligation than to honor the confidence of every parent? More profound responsibilities I cannot imagine.

Every day, parents give us their most treasured gifts — their children — confident we will guard their safety, nourish their souls, stimulate their minds and inspire their imaginations. It is that sacred trust we must honor. It is that sacred trust which explains why teaching is a calling, not just a career. It is that sacred trust that makes clear why we don't need to make a change in the world to make a difference in the world.

The promise of the future, the promise of our students, the promise of our art, the promise of our world depends upon those who teach. For we are the guardians of *those we teach* as much as *what we teach*. Three *little* words indeed. ■

"YES, IF..."

I spend a lot of time in airplanes. My travels have me up in the sky far more than any sane person should be. But even with all that time in the air, and despite the fact I have a private pilot's license and learned all the theory behind *how it works*, not a flight goes by on one of those jumbo jets where I don't marvel at the fact that it does. How can a couple of comparatively small engines lift, let alone keep, ninety collective tons of metal, fiberglass, plastic — and those little bags of pretzels or peanuts — soaring in the sky? Really now, how can that be?

More important, why would anyone propose we do it, let alone think it possible in the first place? I'm telling you, if Wilbur and Orville Wright had come to me back in the days when they were trying to get manned flight "off the ground" I would have given them fifty reasons why it couldn't have worked. Less than a century later, even though modest-sized jet airplanes filled the skies, designers wanted to create airplanes so large they could only be described as flying fortresses weighing well over three-quarters of a million pounds, each capable of carrying half a dozen symphony orchestras at a time with room for their choruses to boot. And you know what? They did it. How? How can that much weight lift from the earth and traverse the heavens with abandon? Far more important than the *how* of it working is the *how* of those who willed it to happen. How did they make the unfathomable possible? In my mind, the answers to each of those questions are intimately related. Let me explain.

Let's pretend I was back with Wilbur and Orville when they decided they wanted to be birds, or at least fly like them. There we are sitting around their bicycle shop in Dayton, Ohio when Orville says, "So, Peter, we're thinking of building a flying machine that can take a man soaring through the skies. Do you think it can work?"

My immediate answer would have been, "*No, because* it will never be sturdy enough to withstand those stresses, falling apart before it ever leaves the ground. *No, because* even if it didn't fall apart, you would have no control of the airplane rolling left or right and it would crash. *No, because* even if you could control the banking of the airplane left and right you still couldn't control the pitch of the nose moving up or down. *No, because* even if that didn't happen you would never get enough sustained lift to fight the power of gravity so you would plummet back to earth. *No, because* even if you solved that you could never stop the yaw of the airplane and it would go into an uncontrollable slip. *No, because* even if that weren't the result there is no design for an airplane propeller that works, and finally *no, because* an engine powerful enough to provide the necessary speed for sustained flight would be far too heavy to allow the airplane to get off the ground. So no, it can never work!"

There you have it, the pursuit of manned flight ended in one brief conversation. Without a doubt, if I were there that day and the Wright brothers listened to me, we would still be dreaming of flight, convinced man would never fly. Why? Because I was an *inhibitor*, serving to convince those visionary brothers that failure was not just possible, it was assured. Using the language of an inhibitor, starting every sentence with "No, because," I succeeded in dooming dreams-of-what-had-never-been-achieved to the realm of the impossible. The unlikely became the unattainable, the hopeful became the hopeless, the promising became the unrealistic.

I would have surely destroyed the spirits of even the most optimistic inventor. Here, as is often the case, *defending why something is not possible is far easier than figuring out how to make that very same thing possible.*

What was so different during those historic days *without me* there to inhibit the Wright brothers? Well the true greatness of Wilbur and Orville rested in their perseverance and indomitable spirit, but even more important was their ability to *enable* their efforts. They were far less interested in why manned flight had not been achieved and far more interested in what manned flight could be.

My guess is the conversation between those bold visionaries probably went something like this: "So, Orville, let's talk about our dream of building a flying machine that can take a man soaring through the skies. Do you think it can work?" To which Wilbur replied, "*Yes, if* we figure out a way to build it sturdy enough to withstand the stresses of takeoff so it doesn't fall apart before it ever leaves the ground. *Yes, if* we invent a way to control the airplane rolling left or right so it won't crash after liftoff. *Yes, if* we come up with a way to control the pitch of the airplane making it possible to aim the nose up and down. *Yes, if* we develop a way to create

enough lift to fight the power of gravity so we won't plummet back to earth once we are airborne. *Yes, if* we devise a
way to stop the sideways yaw movement of the airplane's
tail so we prevent an uncontrollable slip. *Yes, if* we design a
propeller which effectively pulls the aircraft forward, and
finally *yes, if* we build an engine powerful enough to provide
the necessary speed for takeoff and sustained flight yet light
enough to allow the airplane to get off the ground. So yes,
it can absolutely work!"

What really was the difference? Was it just a matter of
semantics? I don't think so. In the words of Harrison Price,
a significant figure in making the dreams of Walt Disney
a reality, "'Yes, if…' is the language of an enabler." Those
words, *that language*, pointing "to what needed to be done
to make the possible plausible." Whereas, "No, because…"
inhibits progress, "Yes, if…" paves the way for it.

As Napoleon Hill so clearly put it, "Whatever the mind
of man can conceive and believe, it can achieve." The language of an enabler helps people to conceive and believe so
they *can* achieve by simply describing what must be done
next. The language of an inhibitor convinces people the
goal is impossible because the path to it is catastrophically
overwhelming. To the inhibitor, defeat is not only possible,
it is a foregone conclusion, warranting no further effort or
thought. To the enabler, success is not only possible with
the steps toward it clearly in focus, it is assured. So the
Wright brothers, enablers both, set out to make their dream
come true by solving one concern at a time, secure of the
outcome at the core.

With each confident "yes, if" of their journey, they
answered the question or solved the problem, with that

spirit inspiring their actions toward answering why it could not be done. By simply working from their success in bicycle design and much trial and error, they figured out better methods to make an airplane's construction sturdier.

One day, while twisting a long thin box in his hands, Wilbur came up with the idea to use a series of cables to control the raising or lowering of each wing with a system he called "wing-warping." This warping or twisting of the wings allowed the airplane to safely bank to the left or right, controlling the rolling movement of the plane.

Next they discovered that by using a movable horizontal surface called an elevator, they could control the pitch of their craft, making it nose up or down as desired.

To find a way to create and sustain enough lift to fight the power of gravity, the brothers tested over two hundred wing shapes, or airfoils, in a wind tunnel until they found the one which produced the most lift.

To solve the problem of the airplane sliding or skidding sideways, the yaw motion which made it difficult to control the craft in a turn, a movable rudder with its own controls replaced the fixed tail. This provided the ability to point the nose of the airplane left or right, preventing uncontrollable slips or skids while warping the wings.

Realizing that an airplane's propeller had to function like a rotating wing, they designed the first effective airplane propeller, able to pull the aircraft forward with great power.

Unable to find an engine powerful enough to provide the necessary speed for takeoff and to keep the airplane aloft once airborne — also light enough to allow the airplane to get off the ground — Wilbur and Orville decided to design and build their own lightweight yet robust one.

Basically, the Wright brothers willed this dream to happen by inventing each technology or system needed to solve each successive step toward their goal. Their beginning mindset provided no preconceived barriers to stop progress before it happened; rather it simply identified what needed to be accomplished for each step as they moved closer to accomplishing what they set out to do.

Can I prove that either Wilbur or Orville Wright ever once uttered the two words — "Yes, if" — as they changed the course of history? No. Though I am sure the spirit of that expression led them to accomplish what others gave up on, others who started with a litany of phrases that began with "No, because."

But I am certain that for a child who is lacking the courage of Wilbur and Orville, less driven or motivated, more frightened or insecure, the words they hear from us, the attitude we convey, the steps for success versus reasons for failure matter greatly. In the classroom, couldn't we agree that even the most dedicated student would just plain "give up" if confronted with an inhibitor, irrespective of how well-intentioned that teacher may be? Conversely, how could that same student help but be caught up in the groundswell of confidence and encouraging plan of action set out by the enabling teacher?

Where inhibitors give reasons why something can't be done, enablers give reasons why it will be done. As teachers we decide whether a student will think "I would if I could, but *I can't* so *I won't*," or "I would if I could, and *I can* so *I will*." They are not just words, they are prophecies.

Tennessee Williams affirmed, "The future is called 'perhaps,' which is the only possible thing to call the future.

And the important thing is not to allow that to scare you."
As teachers we often control whether the future scares our
students into giving up before they even start or inspires
them to continue since their success is assured. As Antoine
de Saint-Exupéry so eloquently wrote, "When it comes to
the future, our task is not to foresee it, but rather to enable
it to happen."

We decide whether our students will believe the words
of Bernard Edmonds: "To dream anything that you want
to dream. That is the beauty of the human mind. To do
anything that you want to do. That is the strength of the
human will. To trust yourself to test your limits. That is
the courage to succeed." We decide whether our students
succeed because they *didn't know they couldn't*. We decide
whether our students embrace the spirit of Robert Louis
Stevenson's profound sentiment: "To be what we are, and to
become what we are capable of becoming, is the only end
of life."

For our students, quite simply, our thinking and acting
like enablers may not change *the* world, but it can change
their world. Can we really do that? *Yes, if...* ■

"THE GREAT ONE"

It began like any other honors band festival: ninety-four young people coming together from far and near, remarkable teachers preparing every detail with the excitement and promise of what could be in the air.

All groups of students we are allowed to stand in front of are special and wonderful in their own way. It is up to us to find their gifts and potential as we help them achieve heights they can't yet imagine possible, and this group was no different. As we started rehearsing it was obvious that individually, each of these young people possessed great skill, a wonderful work ethic and a commitment to their art. But as the hours passed I watched as those ninety-four human beings became an *ensemble*, one enormous force of beauty.

Surely that is our goal and it is the miracle that happens in rehearsal rooms every day, but this time was special. It was more obvious, almost palpable. Or maybe, just maybe, this time I simply took the time to observe it more, relish it more, cherish it more, appreciate it more. I guess it's like the natural beauty around us, or the special people in our lives; sometimes we just don't take the time to notice the things that matter. But this time I did notice and with each passing minute it seemed they became more connected, more drawn together. They melded into a single entity capable of creating emotion, passion and power far greater than any individual.

Over the course of several days of rehearsals I tried to describe the magic that was their melding to a common purpose. I looked for a way to express to them how they came together as one, what they accomplished as a sum far greater than any part and what the joy they shared meant to me. But for all intents and purposes, words failed me. I never really could say what needed to be said.

After the final rehearsal, with many hours before the performance, my thoughtful and gracious host offered to drive me around the region, allowing me to take in some of the natural wonder all around us. We saw beauty beyond compare, views that were indescribable and sights that took your breath away. Then, as I stared off into the distance, it hit me. I realized at that moment how much like mountains, yes mountains, those remarkable students were.

You see, far off in the distance in one direction was Mount McKinley — *Denali* — "The Great One," as it is called, magnificent in its singular grandeur as a peak soaring to the heavens, a peak alone in its greatness, surrounded by seeming foothills. But right in front of my eyes stood the Chugach Mountains, a range of breathtakingly profound beauty and overwhelming majesty not because of any one peak — none coming even close to the height of *Denali* — but because of their vast number. As far as the eye could see, mountain after mountain, peak after peak pushing to the sky, none vying to be the highest, rather each contributing to a brilliant vision, a stunning vista scarcely able to be captured by sight, impossible to be described in words.

I finally had my way of describing what I wanted to make them understand but then I realized I really didn't need to anymore. It was unnecessary. Why try to describe the beauty of a mountain when you are looking right at it? Those kids became the Chugach Mountains. They "got it," they understood. But now I had a new problem. I now had more questions than answers. How does it occur? Why does it happen? What can we do to help it happen? Why does it happen faster with some students and slower with other students? Why is it easier in some years and harder in other years?

I guess we all help our students achieve that sense of ensemble in our own ways; ways as varied as the mountains I saw. It might be through imagery to understand the context of a supporting line, explanations of how individual parts contribute to technical details, or discussions of programmatic threads. It might be our focusing attention on buried treasures of beauty found in accompanying passages, fostering an awareness of the power of suspensions and passing tones, or continued questioning to focus listening around the room. It might be working on the basics of unifying a balanced corporate tone, or developing an ensemble's ability to shape a phrase as one, articulate as one, and emote as one.

Maybe it's playing a passage without the melody, to help find the hidden beauty of a well-crafted accompaniment so its importance becomes vivid. Maybe it's rehearsing sections of a composition without any "first" parts playing, working to develop greater independence of the performers. Maybe it's having parts which create a composite rhythm play together to make the interdependency clear.

Maybe it's working on rounding off a release with elegance
to raise the bar of how inspired their performance can be,
or listening for fragments of a melody hidden in the texture
of a work. It is a constant struggle. But with creative teaching that helps students learn what to do, creates a greater
sense of urgency about how important it is, provides a
heightened awareness of the facets that make the whole,
and raises expectations of achievement, those mountains
will happen.

"The Great One" is indeed in Alaska, and though we
may not have its peak as the view from our classroom,
something greater, *far greater*, happens in every rehearsal
in every city, town or village where individuals gather to
create beauty. Those remarkable young people reminded
me of that, and taught me that Alaska *is* the wonder people
describe it to be, but for far better reasons than could ever
meet the eye. I will not soon forget those students, the magnificence of their home, or the greatness that was them.

JAKE, JOHNNY AND A LESSON WELL LEARNED

O ne of my first teaching experiences was offering beginning band and instrumental lessons in a very small elementary school. More specifically, in the *boiler room* of a very small elementary school. Now I know many of you may have taught in a boiler room, but my boiler was bigger than your boiler. For you see in this tiny school was a furnace slightly larger than the one needed to heat the surface of the sun. It was enormous, slightly older than Moses, and when it kicked on shook the room while making noises similar to a revving 747 aircraft on takeoff. But the best part was when it started up and blew black soot from a small vent on its side.

Small group lessons were a sight to behold: a gaggle of fourth graders working on deep-breathing exercises as a cloud of smoke billowed past them. I feared we would all finish the year with black lung disease. And if the soot wasn't bad enough I could barely hear them make a sound over the rumble of what seemed like centuries-old grinding steel from this boiler first installed in that school when George Washington was in beginning band. It was horrible in ways I just can't describe.

Well this went on for a few weeks until I just couldn't take it anymore. It had to stop. So I went up to the principal's office, knocked on her door and asked if we could speak. She invited me in, wondering what was on my mind. I proceeded to tell her that I could not continue to teach in the boiler room, that it was an impossible situation and that I had to be moved. After I vented for a few minutes, she put her hand up in the air like a stop sign and interrupted me. "Peter," she said, "great teachers can teach anywhere. So go back to your boiler room and be a great teacher." Instantly I was defused, disarmed, dejected and depressed. Crestfallen, I scuffed back to my room unable to muster another word, not smart enough to find a retort to rebut those paralyzing words. So back to my lessons I went, complete with clouds of soot and accompaniments of rumbling machinery.

As the days went on I got angrier and more disillusioned. I finally decided I could take it no longer. One of us—the boiler or me—had to go. So I decided I would march into the principal's office and threaten to quit, before I realized she might just take me up on the offer! Then it hit me. I had what might just be a solution.

I made my way back to the principal's office, knocked on her door and told her I had a problem. She looked straight into my eyes and said, "Not that boiler room thing again, I thought we settled that." "No," I replied, "the problem is me." Looking puzzled, she asked what I meant. "I can't do it," I said. Looking even more puzzled, she queried, "Do what?" I went on to answer, "I have this one lesson group of clarinet students I can't reach. I can't connect with them and I just don't know what to do. I need help." Now looking more concerned than baffled, she immediately offered to help. "When's the next time you'll see them?" she inquired. "Tomorrow morning at nine o'clock," I replied with a pensive voice. "Then I'll be there," she said, "and we'll see what's wrong." My head hanging low, my face showing great concern, I thanked her and walked out of the office.

Once out of sight, I zoomed to the custodian's office to find Jake, our head custodian. As luck would have it I walked into the room and there he was. "Jake," I said with a respectful air of seriousness, "I need a favor." Always willing to help in any way, he said, "What do you need?" I replied, "Jake, I need the furnace to kick on at exactly 9:02 tomorrow morning. Not 9:01 or 9:03, but 9:02 on the dot." His obvious answer was, "Why?" "Better you don't know," I said with a knowing grin, "but can you do it?" He said, "Well yes, but I'm gonna need some help." "Help?" I said, "to turn on a switch?" He said, "Yep, I'm gonna need help from Johnny." Thinking for a moment, knowing we had no custodian by that name, I said, "Johnny? Johnny who?" He said, "Johnny Walker." "The booze?" I replied. He said, "Well, you might call it that." He then went on to say, "If Johnny gets here about 8:30 or so, I bet that boiler would kick on about 9:02."

So I ran to the closest liquor store and bought the biggest bottle of Johnny Walker I could afford, put a note on it that read "9:02 on the dot," and placed it judiciously on Jake's desk in the custodian's office. I then bolted to my room — the boiler room, that is — and proceeded to remove every chair but the eight I needed for the clarinet lesson (and the one for the principal, of course).

The next morning I made sure the boiler room was tidy and neat, or as tidy and neat as a boiler room can be, and checked that the chair count was just right. At about 8:50 my clarinetists arrived and took their seats, readying themselves to play. As I chatted with my students I heard a rap on the open door. Looking up, I welcomed the principal and showed her to her waiting chair which, coincidence of coincidences, happened to be right next to the vent alongside the furnace.

I then began my lesson with some introductory remarks before starting a series of warm-up exercises. Seemingly settled and comfortable, my smiling principal looked around the room, no doubt checking my bulletin boards and all other manner of orderliness. All was fine; students, teacher and principal were doing well.

Staring at the clock like a hawk, I launched into a few deep-breathing exercises at 9:01, working at getting my charges to suck in more and more air. With each passing exercise—and second on the clock—I watched as the big hand moved ever closer to the twelve. With a few seconds to spare I asked the kids to draw in as much air as they could.

Just then, I swear to you, like a bad "B movie" in slow motion, I watched the sweep second hand hit 9:02. At that moment my students prepared to take the deepest breath of their lives as the furnace started up with a thunderous rumble, spewing black soot from its vent. Jake came through. As my young clarinetists sucked in black smoke and began coughing, the principal jumped from her chair, waved her hand to clear the cloud of soot and began yelling, "What *is* that!" With a calm look of nonplussed bewilderment I replied, "What is *what*?" "That noise and all that smoke," she shouted, "what *is* that?" "The boiler," I said with complete composure. "Peter," she authoritatively replied, "this is a totally unsuitable teaching environment. You've got to be moved." "Can you do that?" I asked with a sense of awe. "I can do *anything*," she barked, "I am the principal."

But be careful what you wish for. The next morning I was teaching in the lobby of the gymnasium! No problem teaching breathing; now my biggest challenge was getting kids to play with a steady pulse as they heard fifty basketballs, each dribbling at a different tempo. But I was out of the boiler room and that was all that mattered.

The whole thing is almost incomprehensible: that a music teacher — or any teacher for that matter — would have to teach in a boiler room; that a bottle of spirits could make a furnace come to life; that a principal wouldn't see through such an obvious plan; that a music teacher would have to teach in the lobby of a gymnasium; that teaching in that lobby could be seen as a step up to the finest of facilities; or that a young music teacher would learn one of the most valuable lessons of his life.

For on that day my friend Jake and his friend Johnny taught me a lesson that has served me well for all these years. I most profoundly learned that tact, diplomacy and finesse can get just about anything accomplished, while demands, tantrums and threats almost never do. Now I would be lying if I didn't tell you that deep inside, my knee-jerk reaction is still to "threaten to quit" or some other such manner of throwing a fit, but when I stop and think — *really* think — I always remember Jake, Johnny and that lesson well learned. ▪

SHARE THE GOAL

"So much to teach—so little time." For teachers, could truer words be written? How *much* we must teach to help our students reach the goals we set, and how *well* we must teach it, demand such incredible patience, pacing, planning and perseverance. A casualty, however, of this race against the clock is often one of the most important determining factors of reaching those very goals. Quite simply it's the question of *who* knows what the goal is.

When speaking about this topic to a room full of teachers, I use a simple demonstration to make my point. I stand in front of them, pause in silence, then at the top of my lungs scream the word, "Run!" That's right, in the middle of a crowded room I scream the word "run" with all the power and vehemence I can muster. No matter how many times I do this, no matter where I am, the response never ceases to amaze me. No one moves. No one. In fact my comment to those in attendance is always the same: "Do you realize that not one of you even bothered to uncross your legs, let alone got up and ran?"

Then I try it again with one slight difference. This time I stand in front of them, pause in silence, then proceed to calmly say, "Ladies and gentleman, this auditorium is on fire. You need to *run* to the nearest exit and get outside immediately." Were it not for the fact they knew I was making a point rather than an announcement, you could bet their collective fannies would be out that door before you could blink. Why? Because this time I shared the goal with them so they knew the reason why they should run, saw the value in running and understood the purpose of my asking them to run. Armed with that information they knew why they were running as well as to where they were running.

How many of us can think of countless hours of ensemble rehearsals where our conductor asked us to repeat passages over and over again, never knowing why? Surely the conductor knew why he or she was asking for the passage to be repeated, but we didn't. Not knowing what was wrong with what they did, the performers have no idea what to do to better their performance. How could they possibly fix what's wrong, improve what's not good enough, or solidify what's inconsistent if they didn't know what that was?

As conductors we don't intentionally keep our performers in the dark. I think we either forget to make it a priority or are in such a hurry to get things done that we don't take the time to do it. It is time consuming, but is time well spent. In a rehearsal, like in a crowded auditorium, I won't—no, I really can't—effectively "run" to a goal unless I know what that goal is and why I'm running there.

Will there be times we need to repeat a passage simply so we can have another chance to figure out what's wrong or what we don't like? Will there be times we repeat the work at hand solely with the goal of developing consistency, context, confidence and comfort? Will there be times we want to hear it again just to make sure the last successful playing wasn't luck? Yes, so why not share those goals with performers, for aren't those reasons as important as fixing wrong rhythms or dynamics? To me, any goal expressed to our students, short of something as ridiculous as "make it sound good," is one worth sharing.

When I think about the importance of sharing the goal with our students I remember back to a wind ensemble rehearsal while I was in college. There I was sitting in the trumpet section during a particularly "repetitious" rehearsal. The conductor for the upcoming concert loved to repeat passages over and over and over and over again with little if any feedback as to what we could do to correct or improve things. Somewhere in the middle of this grueling rehearsal, after having repeated the introduction of this piece what seemed to be two or three *thousand* times, my stand partner leaned over to me and said, "Next time, I'm going to play all of the B-naturals as B-flats, you play them as C's and tell the guys on the next stand to play them as C-sharps." I looked at him as if he had lost his mind and asked, "Why?" I'll never forget his answer or the devious look on his face when he said, "At least then we'll know why we have to play it again!"

Being cowards, we never acted out the plot, but boy did we want to, because it really *would* have been nice, at least once, to have known why we were repeating that introduction. Will our students ever get frustrated enough to do something like that? Hopefully not, but if we make certain to share the *why* as much as the *how* and *what* of our directives toward those goals, their progress and growth will be ensured. So the next time you feel the pressure of the clock in a rehearsal, and are tempted to skip those moments of sharing the goal as you hurry toward it, doing the educational equivalent of yelling the word "run," remember that auditorium full of people who never even uncrossed their legs. ■

BROCCOLI

I'm guessing you are trying to figure out what broccoli — yes, that green bulbous vegetable — could possibly have to do with music education or being a better teacher. Well I believe a lot. Let me try to explain.

As teachers, when we are presented with ideas, we can react many different ways, though generally they fall into three broad categories. For example, if I were to present you with a certain technique for teaching rhythm, you would probably have one of three reactions.

The first reaction is agreement: the technique is exactly what you do, we basically agree. We could start a club and start printing t-shirts. The second reaction brings somewhat less agreement, but agreement nonetheless. It may be you did it that way in the past but forgot about it, or you do something very similar, or you would be willing to try it to see if you like it, or you feel aspects of the approach could be blended with your current way. You may not want to join the club but you would wear the t-shirt if it were free.

The third reaction is contempt. As the words describing the technique pass from my lips you are utterly appalled, aghast at what I'm espousing, downright angered by the very thought of what I am suggesting. You not only don't currently do it that way, or anything like that way, but the very idea makes you cringe. You wouldn't use the t-shirt as a dust rag.

Though the first reaction is okay and the second is fine, my favorite is the third. Why, you ask? Well it is always nice to find people who agree on a topic. It helps one confirm the validity and soundness of the idea. But having people strongly disagree means they are as fervent in their beliefs as I am in mine. Disagreements like that make for continued growth and development, challenging each of us to re-evaluate what we think. Even if we end up with the same opinion, the process of testing our viewpoint is so very beneficial.

Without question, the third reaction is wonderful, but only if people do not come to their adamant belief the way my son came to his opinion about broccoli.

You see years ago, when my son Peter was the ripe old age of three or four our family was sitting around the kitchen table for dinner. It was a dinner I will never forget. Holding a large bowl of steamed broccoli, I said, "Peter, would you like some broccoli?" He replied, "No." I asked why. He quite firmly declared, "I hate broccoli." So I said, "You hate broccoli, but have you ever tried it?" To that he incredulously said, "Dad, why would I ever try something that I hate?" Dumbfounded, I looked at my wife and said, "How do you argue with that logic?" Why indeed would anyone try something they hate?

Now you're still wondering what this can possibly have to do with teaching. Well many of us come to our resolute opinions about ideas, techniques or materials the same way my son arrived at his attitude about broccoli. We learned a

way of doing something in college, taught to us by someone we respected, so we have continued to use it to this
day, defending it in our minds as the best way. Sometimes
it becomes so crystallized in our minds that we don't challenge it, seek to modify or improve it, or look for better
ways. We are almost petrified in place, seemingly fearing
lightning bolts from heaven if we dare stray from *that* way.

Certainly those ideas from long ago may be the best
way, leaving you completely justified in your reaction. But
sometimes I fear we take them as the best way only because
someone once told us they were. My hope is that we challenge any belief, verify any information, test any approach
and experiment with new ways to any goal. New ideas *can*
be better and we must be open to trying them. We may
find something we like better and choose to adopt it, not
because it is new, but because we deem it better. Likewise,
some time-tested approaches may be the best way, not
because they are old, but because they work well.

Any idea worth its salt should be able to withstand
challenge. Often challenging tenets we hold dear can be
difficult but challenge them we must. We owe it to our students, our art and ourselves to seek the best approaches to
our goals, defending them because we have reason, real reason, to do so. Remember, if people hadn't challenged what
they had been taught, the medical profession would still be
teaching doctors to bleed patients with leeches.

So the next time you are presented with a new way of
doing something, however peculiar it may seem, remember
my son and his broccoli; more important, remember how
growth and progress more often than not come from the
simple quest to find a better way. If nothing else, what a

wonderful lesson that is for our students to learn from our example. Quite simply, when they see us try new or different ways, test novel ways or challenge our usual ways, they learn that doing so is healthy and constructive. That is a lesson that will serve them well, a lesson far more important than simply trying broccoli. ▓

VISION

Fulton Oursler wrote, "Every day man crucifies himself between two thieves — fear of tomorrow and regrets of yesterday." Worse still, that fear and regret is often so debilitating as to obscure the enjoyment of today — the here and now. In so doing it becomes easy to cloak the past, present and future in a haze of negativity, worry and doubt.

As teachers, however, nothing could be more foreign to our way of thinking. For at the heart of education is the premise that we learn from yesterday, savor today and look forward to tomorrow. That we plan as a result of the past, enjoy and truly live the present, and dream of what the future can hold as a consequence. Quite simply, at the core of being a teacher is that mysterious quality called *vision*: the ability to see more than meets the eye.

Vision is a magical mixture of hindsight, foresight, now-sight and insight that is the essence of great teaching. It is that remarkable combination, in just the right proportion, at just the right time, in just the right way that can make all the difference in the lives of those whom we are entrusted to teach. Just like a marvelous recipe for some fabulous dish, the subtle interplay and balance of every ingredient and cooking technique is seemingly invisible to the uninitiated, but in the hands of a master chef can become a thing of beauty.

Hindsight

Hindsight is simply the ability to look at what has already occurred, to perceive and examine aspects of previous events and decisions as they truly happened, and see other possibilities or choices that could have been more appropriate or beneficial. It is basically the ability to objectively assess the past.

Most people think of hindsight in negative terms, with statements like "well, in hindsight I would never have bought that car" or "in hindsight I guess I should have unplugged the iron." But for teachers, hindsight is a valuable commodity. It is essential, for without it we would have no idea where our students *are*, before starting them on the path to where they are *going*. Hindsight allows us to establish starting points, it is the fruit of assessment, it is the information we need to know to help children *bloom where they are planted*. We are all simply a product of our past.

Though in the process of education "what was" can be viewed with regret and criticism, it is always best to view it rather as a result; facts as we now know them to be. What is, is. What was becomes extraordinarily valuable information we as teachers can use. From that information we can plan future curriculum, tailor specific lessons, learn which approaches work and which fail, assess learning styles, individualize instruction and reflect on our expectations. As teachers, hindsight allows us to live the words of that wonderful old phrase: "We cannot direct the wind...but we can adjust the sails." Or as Joe Pass so succinctly put it, "If you hit a wrong note, then make it right by what you play afterwards."

Hindsight allows us to do just that by assessing what has occurred as much as learning from it, processing what was as much as planning what will be, creating the future from our knowledge of the past. I guess the best analogy for hindsight is rowing a boat. As we row a boat forward, we face backward, always looking where we have been, moving ahead based on what we see behind us. In so doing, moving correctly toward the future by referencing what has been in our past.

It is said that information is power and much of that power comes from what we learn from a keenly developed sense of hindsight.

Foresight

Foresight: the act of looking to the future, providing for the future, understanding the significance of the future, and acting upon the present as a *result* of one's view of the future. Could anything be more "teacher-like"? We look at the past as a springboard or launch pad to the future. Then, using foresight, we envision what our students can be and chart a course for their destiny. In a nutshell, foresight is seeing potential, dreaming of what can be — not what others *say* can be — with the only true limitation to those dreams being *our imaginations*. I often think of foresight as being able to *see even with our eyes closed*: that dreaming, that envisioning of hidden potential, that seeing what's within each of our students that is at the very core of being a teacher. What a wonderful metaphor for teaching. What a wonderful metaphor for so much of life, or more important, living.

As with hindsight, most people think of foresight negatively, with phrases such as "I wish I had the foresight to bring an umbrella." But foresight, true foresight, offers us the opportunity not only to look toward the future as we want it to be, but to create it that way. Foresight allows us to prevent what we *don't* want to happen and to cause or initiate what we *do* want to happen. It allows us to live out of our imaginations instead of our *memories*. More important, it allows us to live out of our imaginations rather than our *regrets*.

Now-Sight

Tennessee Williams wrote, "Life is all memory, except for the one present moment that goes by you so quickly you hardly catch it going." Don't you think it's true many of us go through much of our teaching day, let alone our lives, *looking — but not seeing — because our eyes are closed?* How sad it is when we spend so much time and energy worrying about the past or future that we don't enjoy and savor the moment, the here and now, that we don't see what's there, right in front of us.

It's like holding a camera with hopes of taking the perfect picture. There we are impatiently waiting for the perfect shot, worrying about seizing the right instant, anguishing over opportunities lost. More often than not, though, we spend so much time doing all that, we miss the moment. I don't just mean miss the photograph, I mean miss even seeing — really seeing — the precious scene that just passed unnoticed, unappreciated, unrepeatable.

The problem we teachers have is that we spend so much time focusing on hindsight and foresight that we often don't take the time to live in the moment. Now I know teaching a fourth-grade clarinet lesson about getting over the break or correcting the left wrists of a class of beginner violinists can be maddeningly frustrating, and the only thing that sometimes "gets us through" is focusing on what possibilities lay ahead for those students after they learn those lessons, but we must enjoy the journey as much as the destination. Finding joy along the path to the goal is, quite possibly, more important than savoring joy once the goal has been achieved.

Jonathan Swift hoped for this when he cautioned, "May you live every day of your life." Buddha sought the same ideal when he reasoned, "If we could see the miracle of a single flower clearly, our whole life would change." But Albert Einstein said it most eloquently: "There are two ways to live your life. One is as though nothing is a miracle. The other is as though everything is a miracle." The miracle of living, the miracle of education, the miracle of growth demand that we honor those words by seeing our "now" as much as our "what was" and "what will be."

I guess now-sight boils down to *seeing* versus *looking*, and we alone determine which we will do, how we will spend our days. One thing's for sure, we can never forget that the same seven letters that create the words "the eyes" make the words "they see," but only if we let them, only if we make them and only if we take the time to do so. Right now — this moment — is not simply the space between the past and the future. It is a brief moment that must be treasured and enjoyed.

Insight

Hindsight is contemplating the past to guide the future. Foresight is envisioning the potential the future holds. Now-sight is cherishing the present moment, but the most magical of the four "sights" must be the last one: *insight*. Insight is that ability to look at events with intuition, perception and understanding. It is having an awareness of what motivates students and seeing the underlying truths that govern any situation.

A teacher's insight is part mystic, part pragmatist, part sage, part shaman and part psychologist. Our stock in trade: being as astute as we are ingenious, as skillful as we are clever, possessing judgment as sound as it is nimble. In short it is living the words of William Arthur Ward who said, "The pessimist complains about the wind; the optimist expects it to change; the realist adjusts the sails." As teachers, pessimists wallow in regrets of the past; optimists, without the guidance of information and a plan, hope for improvement; but realists, armed with hindsight and foresight to guide them, can enjoy the now-sight of the present while guiding "the ships" that are our students with the instinct, wisdom and understanding of true insight.

A Teacher's Eyes

Maybe Steve Cook said it best: "Art is not devoid of reason or intellect. It's packed with it. It's just not driven by it. How can I put this? Maybe it's that the artist is like a train riding on the tracks of experience and logic, but the steam which drives him or her is emotion and vision."

For teachers seeing is more than just believing, it's knowing, hoping, envisioning, evaluating, estimating, planning,
growing, cajoling, enjoying and calculating. But above all
it's believing. Believing in the power of education. Believing
in the promise of education.

In so doing let us each resolve to live the following
words of Napoleon Hill: "Cherish your visions and your
dreams as they are the children of your soul; the blueprints
of your ultimate achievements." Remembering all the while
that sometimes the things you can't see matter most. ▧

THE MAGIC OF
CONDUCTING

An artist takes paint to a canvas and brings beauty to the world for all to see. An architect uses a pencil to give shape to buildings that grace our towns. A sculptor molds clay to fashion works of style and substance to enrich minds and hearts. But what does a conductor do? Aren't we basically waving our hands in thin air? If you did that alone on the corner of Main Street and First Avenue in any town you would probably be locked up in a rubber room.

The best answer I have ever found comes from the extraordinary Leonardo da Vinci who referred to the art of music as "the shaping of the invisible." However perfect that description may be for music in general, what better words could describe the elusive art of conducting? It *is* the shaping of the invisible which is what makes it at once exhilarating and frustrating, rewarding and daunting.

So we study and practice in efforts to prepare ourselves to stand on a podium and shape the invisible. We study every mark on the score to further our knowledge and preparedness. We practice every conducting gesture until it is mastered. We know the score cold. But sadly if we stop at that point, that may be a large part of our problem.

To illustrate my point, let me share a passage from Howard Roughan's wonderful novel, *The Promise of a Lie*, in which a college student speaks to his professor about a case-study analysis he had written, asking why he hadn't received a higher grade: "'That's easy,' he told me. 'You only saw what was in front of you.' When I asked what he meant, he asked me — surprise — if I played chess. 'A little,' I lied. 'Then you can appreciate its paradox; how it's a game of infinite possibilities defined by a finite set of movements. That's why, ultimately, chess is played in your head and not on the board in front of you,' he said. 'The board represents the finite. Your head represents the infinite. If you only play what you see, you'll never win. The point is, to excel in chess — and anything else for that matter, including this class — you have to imagine. You have to see beyond what's in front of you.' 'In other words...your paper proved only that you'd read the case. But those who scored higher proved something more. That they'd read *into* the case. They used their heads and saw beyond the facts presented.'"

Knowing the score like the backs of our hands is the first step, and an important one by any measure, but if that is where it stops we end up only knowing the backs of our hands. Surely the study of music theory, music history, performance practice, orchestration and the like will bring a wealth of information to the table. Without question the study of other arts, science, philosophy and history will broaden our view and inform our opinion. But it is only when we use imagination, vision, curiosity, interpretation, wonder and creativity to mold that knowledge that we end up truly making a score our own, making it a part of us, making that *invisible* seem *visible*.

Maybe the best description of this comes from Robert Henri when he advised, "Paint the flying spirit of the bird rather than its feathers." How often do we conduct a perfect fermata, a flawless crescendo or a pristine cue that is scarcely more than brush strokes of correct information, doing little to help shape the invisible qualities that make the music fly, dance or weep? How often do our gestures paint accurate brush strokes of technique that do little to capture the spirit of the work?

Unquestionably good technique is important and a given, for if my brush strokes look more like a horse than a bird, it really doesn't matter whether I was trying to capture the flying spirit or the feathers, it still looks like a horse. I have failed at both. But secure and exceptional technique should only be a tool that allows us to see further and envision more.

Bringing all we know, all we are and all we can imagine to our conducting makes for technique which is so much a part of the organic nature of a work that the strokes of a brush are not seen, only that flying spirit. It is no longer an interpretation of a composition but us living through the piece and the piece living through us.

As Bruce Adolph so perfectly stated in his book, *What to Listen for in the World*, "When a musician is convinced of what a piece should be, how it should sound, what it means, when a musician feels she has discovered the essence of a work, she identifies with it, embodies it, then she does not think that her performance is an interpretation: it is the piece as the composer meant it to be." "To play just the first note of a phrase, a performer must know context — like an actor entering upon a scene: What is the setting? What do I want? Am I prepared for what is about to happen? Should I be surprised? Where have I been? What is my mood, my energy, my pulse, my direction?" He goes on to say, "Before any sound, there is already meaning." "False music displays. True music reveals. Any kind of music may be invented. True music sounds discovered."

It is that depth of understanding, creative realization, comfort through confidence and impassioned discovery that allows us to shape the invisible and more important harness the willingness, excitement and talents of those we conduct to join us in that endeavor. Not that our words demand it but rather that our intensity, enthusiasm and grasp of the material command it. In that way we make every performer part of the process, a companion on the journey. As Alberto Suarez so aptly put it, "A lot of conductors come in and they interpret the piece for you. But great conductors interpret the piece with you."

What follows are a few thoughts toward that end. Ideas to help free us from that which holds us back, ideas to allow us to be the conductor we want to be, and, even better, the conductor we want our students to have.

Conducting as Archery

It may seem odd to relate the sport of archery to the art of conducting, but let me explain. Many years ago while at a Renaissance Fair with my children we attended an archery demonstration. Several talented archers thrilled the audience with feats of precision that were nothing short of amazing.

Time after time, whether shooting from short distances or what seemed the length of a football field, every arrow met its intended target. As I sat there in awe of the skill these people possessed, one of them spoke about two different philosophies of archery, "point and aim" and "instinctive."

He then demonstrated each approach. First he showed the point-and-aim technique by holding the bow and arrow steady, firmly, methodically as he took slow and careful aim at the target. His concentration was palpable. You could feel the tension as he readied to shoot. Finally after what seemed to be an eternity of aiming, he let loose his arrow for its trip to the absolute center of the target. It was impressive.

Then he demonstrated instinctive technique by fixing an arrow to the bow, pointing the arrow in the general direction of the target, pulling back his arm and letting the arrow fly in what felt like a millisecond in total. By the time I had processed what he had done the arrow had likewise pierced the bull's-eye of the target. Though the point and aim demonstration was still impressive, the instinctive demonstration was utterly mind-boggling. It was as if he wasn't even looking at the target, let alone aiming precisely. It was as if he didn't really even need to see the target, as if the arrow just knew where to go. It was effortless, fluid, nonchalant and perfect.

Was the point-and-aim shot any less perfect? No, but it was anything but effortless or nonchalant. It was a wonderful display of technique for all to see. We in the audience were captivated by every moment of the skill used to get that arrow to the target, whereas with the instinctive shot, we simply marveled at the arrow resting firmly in the center of the target before we even realized the archer had made the shot. One approach featured the technique to get the arrow there, the other approach simply that the arrow *was* there.

At that moment I appreciated the similarities between archery and conducting as my mind flooded with questions. Do our gestures draw attention to the musical result of the gesture or the mechanics of the gesture itself? Does our conducting look effortless or does it look contorted, fluid or mechanical, nonchalant or forced? Have we internalized the music so much that the gestures used to create it look as if they *are the music* or do they look like they are efforts to direct traffic? Do we need to deliberately point and aim every movement we make or are those motions so much a part of us, and so much a part of the music, that we *instinctively* move? Do we know the rules that govern good conducting technique—what a certain gesture elicits and why—so we know when those rules can or should be broken? Have we made our conducting so much a part of us that it truly serves the music and our musicians?

Every time I conduct I think of that archer, his demonstration and the lesson he taught me. I know ability like that comes from finely honed skill and technique, but his was so profound as to be made invisible by his confidence, grace and elegance. A goal I think we all share every time we step on a podium.

Habits

"Habit is either the best of servants," stated Nathaniel Emmons, "or the worst of masters." When it comes to conducting that is surely true. Our habits are either tried and true friends that allow us to move with assuredness or they are villains waiting around every corner. In reality, habits are neither good nor bad. It is whether they are intended or not that characterizes them. I think we would all agree the habit of looking both ways before crossing the street is a good one, and the habit of riding the brake while driving is a bad one. Just as the habit of our looking at the performers rather than the score is a good one and regularly counting off to start an ensemble is a bad one.

Will we all agree on whether a habit is good or bad? No, but I'm sure we can agree that we want to rid ourselves of what we perceive as our bad habits and encourage the development of what we want to have as good habits. The best way I know to help make good gestures become habitual or stop bad gestures from being habitual is to borrow a concept from the teaching of language.

It is the notion of active and passive vocabulary. To help students make a certain word part of their common usage, a habit if you will, they are instructed to *intentionally use* it five times, making it part of their active vocabulary. Whereas to help them rid a certain word from usage, they are instructed to *intentionally not use* it five times, forcing it to become part of their passive vocabulary.

As conductors we can use the same process to make specific good gestures habitual by intentionally using them when possible and appropriate in an effort to make them our own. But more important we can help stop the use of gestures we deem bad habits by intentionally not using them when we instinctively — habitually — would have wanted to. Simply making our use of good habits a conscious choice will eventually make them part of our active conducting vocabulary, as consciously choosing not to use our bad habits will force them to retreat to our passive conducting vocabulary.

Flow by Design

In an effort to explain his remarkable abilities, the legendary ice hockey player Wayne Gretzky said, "I skate to where the puck is going to be, not where it has been." Think about it: the difference between good hockey players and great hockey players often rests in their intuitive, instinctive, almost magical ability to be where the puck ends up, just at the moment that it does.

In conducting that translates to the flow of our motions, the choreography of our gestures from one to the next, seamlessly moving as we shape the invisible. Beyond making every gesture a part of us by the music flowing through us we must practice and plan our conducting so gestures seem to give way one to the next with unending fluidity. If every gesture comes to the fore or retreats to the background with elegance and precision — our hands knowing where they need to be before they arrive there — our portrayal will seem as intuitive and instinctive as when the great Gretsky arrived where the puck was to be before *it* even seemed to know it.

Now before we go any further, I must admit to you that I possess the athletic ability of a blueberry, and the extent of my knowledge about sports can comfortably be written on the head of a pin. But watching the movements, timing and graceful motions of great athletes, like great dancers, can provide a model often not that far afield (pardon the pun!) from great conducting.

Stop the Jabbering

Many years ago, I designed a class for my graduate conducting students to help them with several aspects of conducting that weren't really conducting, but were equally valuable. The class delved into *tai chi*, mime, sign language, acting, public speaking, Alexander Technique and dance. An expert in each field taught his or her subject and then helped integrate those skills into conducting. With each passing topic it became apparent how valuable it was to the study of conducting. And though the study of all of them was extremely beneficial, the correlation and similarities between the art of mime and conducting seemed most vivid.

From the fluid sequencing of movements to the planned use or lack of use of specific gestures, from the stillness of the canvas before one starts to the use of proportion, consistency and intensity, mimes are conductors as surely as conductors are mimes. So I urge you to study the art of mime and see for yourself how it impacts your every movement, enlightens your mind and nourishes your soul. Though almost every aspect of a mime's art can relate to conducting, I would like to address two specific areas I found especially helpful: jabbering and repetition.

Quite simply jabbering is when a mime does a lot of movements without communicating much of anything. Call it gibberish, babbling or noise, it is useless to the portrayal at hand. When much is done with the hands, body and face, but little is communicated, it is as valueless to the art of mime as it is to the art of conducting. A few targeted, specific movements that "speak" volumes to a mime's audience always trump many motions that "say" nothing. As conductors we just as assuredly suffer from this problem when much is conducted but little is expressed or conveyed to our performers.

Repetition is another enormous problem shared by mimes and conductors. For both, some repetition may be good for providing emphasis or clarification, but mind-numbing repetition of movements or gestures does little but lull those watching into a state of boredom, making them less attuned to important communications or subtle nuances. If a conductor constantly pounds every beat of every pattern, it ends up meaning nothing. Then when a true accent is needed on a downbeat, communicating that becomes most difficult. It's like a car alarm. At first it is noticed but after a while it's simply ignored. As conductors, like mimes, we must guard against unnecessary repetition which creeps into our conducting without our even know-ing it, just as much as we are aware of jabbering that says nothing.

Context

Hanging on the wall in my office is a wonderful copy of an antique photograph. It shows an old biplane crashed into, and just hanging in, an old tree. That portion of the photo is a sad sight but not entirely strange. However the rest of the photo shows a barren wasteland for miles on end, with not a single other tree — or anything else for that mat-ter — for as far as the eye can see. It is that context, that perspective which makes the picture odd. The incongruity of that one plane in that one tree with no other obstacles in view that makes it bizarre to say the least.

In that same way every musical moment of a piece, and every gesture we conduct, can be perceived differently by the context of what surrounds it. The raspy tone of a straight-muted trumpet may seem violent when surrounded by the serene sounds of a subtle clarinet chorale, but may be wholly unnoticed as part of a bombastic percussion interlude. It's simply context.

Likewise a powerful jabbing conducting gesture may communicate volumes if it interrupts a sensitive passage to emulate the vibrant blast of a bass-drum strike, but would probably be disregarded if that gesture were to be one of many redundant gestures.

A crashed airplane on the ground when seen amongst many piled in a junkyard has one meaning; that lone biplane resting in the only tree in sight, an entirely different one. Neither better nor worse, just different simply by what surrounds them.

Remember the Magic

Through it all, the technique, the gestures, the analysis and the facts, the most important aspect of conducting is the one no words can describe. It is the magic, the human connection, the soul only a person can bring to the podium. It is the power of one's musical conviction, one's spiritual essence, which defies description or logic. It is that sharing of ourselves, of who we are, with all those whom we teach. As Carl Jung so eloquently said, "Your vision will become clear only when you can look into your own heart. Who looks outside, dreams; who looks inside, awakens."

As we awaken, as conductors, as teachers, as human beings maybe we can do no better than to follow the advice of Marcus Aurelius who reminded each of us, "Dig within. Within is the wellspring of good; and it is always ready to bubble up, if you just dig." A wellspring of artistry and emotions we must then show to all those whom we touch. A wellspring that will serve each of our students as a beacon, a model, a guide. Each of us must search our hearts, souls and minds for the best we have, for our art and our students deserve nothing less. As Dom Famularo simply put it, "Find that river that runs deep within you. Find a way to tap into it, and let the essence of who you are flow freely for the world to see."

Maybe J. K. Rowling's character Albus Dumbledore in *Harry Potter and the Sorcerer's Stone* stated it better than anyone ever could when he said, "Ah music, a magic beyond all we do here!" Through it all let us never forget that magic.

THE REAL VOYAGE

"You see this goblet?" asks Achaan Chaa, the Thai meditation master. "For me this glass is already broken. I enjoy it; I drink out of it. It holds my water admirably, sometimes even reflecting the sun in beautiful patterns. If I should tap it, it has a lovely ring to it. But when I put this glass on the shelf and the wind knocks it over or my elbow brushes it off the table and it falls to the ground and shatters, I say, 'Of course.' When I understand that the glass is already broken, every moment with it is precious."

How many of us—through frustration with where our students *are* versus where we know we want them to be; or because our dedication drives us never to settle, but rather always to push our students to the next step—don't cherish the time we have with our students? That remarkable quote from Mark Epstein's *Thoughts Without A Thinker* puts it all in perspective. Many of us dwell so much on where our students should be by the end of the year, or by concert or contest time, that we forget they all too soon will be gone. That wonderful, unique group of individuals will move on in only months. That thought helps us to think of each of our moments with our students as precious. As the goblet thought of as already broken is treasured, time with our students must be savored.

Put succinctly by H. Satchel, "Happiness is not having what you want, but rather wanting what you have." I know it's sometimes hard to think of that when we hear sounds that aren't recognizable as Western art music but we can never be truly happy until we do. Otherwise we will always be waiting for happiness — or that day when we *can* cherish time with our students — sometime in the future. As former President Ronald Reagan stated, "Don't wait until the evening sunset to see the beauty of the day." Work toward that majestically beautiful sunset but enjoy every ray of sun and yes, every storm cloud that passes.

If you only cherish the time with groups that are stellar, or the times that produce great results, you will get to the end of a career with far fewer moments of joy than if you follow those incredible words of Herb Gardner: "You have got to own your days and name them, each one of them, every one of them, or else the years go right by and none of them belong to you." Don't let the years just *go* by. Cherish every second of every day, and name each of them with the smiles of joy or looks of amazement on the faces of those whom you teach. Maybe it is simply realizing that "the real voyage of discovery," as Marcel Proust so perfectly stated, "consists not in seeking new landscapes, but in having new eyes."

Acting on that thought is certainly more of a challenge with some children than with others. Savoring moments with students who seem uninterested or unfocused is hard. It helps to keep in mind the truth of J. R. R. Tolkien's "The Riddle of Aragorn" from *The Fellowship of the Ring*: "Not all those who wander are lost." No one, no matter how wonderful a teacher he or she is, can *always* know whether children who appear to be wandering are really lost. Maybe they are, or maybe they are processing, imagining, extrapolating or analyzing. Just maybe that moment a student *looks* lost could be a moment of revelation: the moment "the light finally went on."

We can be the teacher who nurtures those moments. We can be the teacher who fosters what is truly important in a young person's life. We can be the teacher who always teaches life lessons as well as music lessons, sending the true message that every child needs to learn, best stated by the remarkable Pablo Casals: "Each second we live in a new and unique moment of the universe, a moment that never was before and will never be again. And what do we teach our children in school? We teach them that two and two make four, and that Paris is the capital of France. When will we also teach them what they are? We should say to each of them: Do you know what you are? You are a marvel. You are unique. In all of the world there is no other child exactly like you. In the millions of years that have passed there has never been another child like you. And look at your body — what a wonder it is! Your legs, your arms, your cunning fingers, the way you move! You may become a Shakespeare, a Michelangelo, a Beethoven. You have the capacity for anything. Yes, you are a marvel. And when you grow up, can you then harm another who is, like you, a marvel? You must cherish one another. You must work — we all must work — to make this world worthy of its children."

Those words of Casals are as brilliant as the music he created. Now *that* is a life lesson! But it is also a tall order. How does one even start? For me, I start by trying every day to work toward cherishing and being worthy of the children I teach. Will I ever truly be? Probably not, but all any of us can do is try. All any of us can do is live the words of Rachel Carson: "If a child is to keep alive his inborn sense of wonder, he needs...at least one adult who can share it, rediscovering with him the joy, excitement and mystery of the world we live in." We may be the only adult who does, so we must. A friend of mine once said that a truly great music teacher "always puts the students first, the music second and themselves last."

Is that easy? No, but as Tom Brokaw affirmed, "It's easy to make a buck. It's a lot harder to make a difference." Think of those teachers who made a difference in your life. Think of the true lessons they taught you. For me, every one of them cared more about me as a person than about anything they hoped to teach me and worked as hard to make me a better human being as they did to make me a smarter student.

Mitch Albom in his stunning book, *Tuesdays with Morrie*, chronicled the life and death of one such teacher of his. I think we can live no better than to strive to exemplify his words: "Have you ever really had a teacher? One who saw you as a raw but precious thing, a jewel that, with wisdom, could be polished to a proud shine? If you are lucky enough to find your way to such teachers, you will always find your way back. Sometimes it is only in your head. Sometimes it is right alongside their beds. The last class of my old professor's life took place once a week, in his home, by a window in his study where he could watch a small hibiscus plant shed its pink flowers. The class met on Tuesdays. No books were required. The subject was the meaning of life. It was taught from experience. The teaching goes on."

But how does one *teach* the meaning of life? Well, by showing and "being" the simple credo of Jonathan Swift: "May you live all the days of your life." Indeed. May you — and every student you touch — remember to *enjoy* the precious moments shared, *want* what you have, *name* every day, *have* new eyes, *make* a difference, *cherish* one another, and truly *live* all the days of your life.

THE INVISIBLE
CONNECTION

As teachers we have so many goals. High among them would have to be our desire to connect with our students—each of our students—in a deep, profound, meaningful way. It's about forming an invisible connection with them in every rehearsal: developing an intense bond between every member of the ensemble and ourselves. A bond the likes of which can only come from the eyes. I think of it as thin beams of light which pass from our eyes to each performer's eyes. Through that invisible yet intensely powerful connection, we communicate. I envision one hundred, or fifty, or thirty silk-thin beams of light, one coming from each of our student's eyes all focused on our eyes. Then from us comes a beam of light directed right back to each of them.

The stronger the connection, the more meaningful the communication. Communication through which *we* share our passion, love, satisfaction, frustration, disappointment, enjoyment, pride and sense of wonder. More important, communication through which *our students* share *their* passion, love, satisfaction, frustration, disappointment, enjoyment, pride and sense of wonder.

We develop that connection by sharing ourselves with our students, not just our time and knowledge, but our spirit and soul; by making that connection an essential aspect of our expectations, never settling for less; and by conditioning our ensemble members to make those connections. Yes, conditioning. In many ways, just like training a mouse or puppy, we condition our students' *communication* behavior no less than their classroom-discipline behavior.

We all know it's fairly easy, with patience and a plan, to *intentionally* condition behaviors in our students to help them be successful. However it's just as easy to *unintentionally* condition them to do things we don't want or, even worse, things which are counterproductive to our goal, without our even knowing we are doing it!

In addition, that conditioning goes both ways. Our students can condition *us* just as easily, reminding me of the wonderful words of George Carlin: "The truth is, Pavlov's dog trained Pavlov to ring his bell just before the dog salivated." As our behavior helps shape our students' behavior, so too does their behavior shape ours. By way of example let's say our third clarinet players never look up in rehearsal, but those playing first clarinet look up all the time. It's easy to fall into the habit of ignoring the third clarinets, since they're not watching anyway, focusing all our attention on the first clarinets who watch so well. We will have been conditioned by those third clarinet players never to look at them. If we don't take the necessary steps to train *them* to watch, they will succeed in *training us* to disregard them. So who's training whom?

A few years ago, after giving a workshop on how to get an ensemble to watch, I received a letter from a music teacher that described this conditioning process perfectly. I immediately asked his permission to share this dedicated teacher's experience and wisdom with you here. The story began with the revelation he had not only trained his students *to not look up*, but to be *afraid to look up*. That's right, afraid to look at their conductor. He went on to describe how *unintentional* conditioning *caused* the problem, but far more important, how *intentional* conditioning *solved* the problem.

> About two years ago, I was a "score staring" conductor, never looking up at anyone (well, almost never) while I rehearsed. The downbeat came, and my eyes went with it. I don't know why I did it; maybe I was so intent on listening that I couldn't look up. Maybe I was afraid that when I looked up I wouldn't be affirmed in what I was doing. I stared down at the music until I heard something I wasn't supposed to hear (talking, mutes dropping, a squeak). Then, I would look up, find the person who made the offending noise, and give them the patented "teacher stare" that says "I know what you did, and if you do it again, God have mercy on your soul!"
>
> Well, I gradually realized that I wasn't looking at them (and vice versa) and the group and I were totally divorced from the musical experience we were having every day. It was like we were in those "iso" booths in a recording studio, having the same musical experience, yet totally cut off from each other. I started noticing when students came up to me before or after class, they rarely looked me in the eye. I had thoroughly conditioned them that eye contact was akin to negative reinforcement, and it took months of retraining to turn it around.
>
> That began with me looking at them warm up before the rehearsal started. I would just watch them take their seats and get ready. I would purposely try not to react to anything going on....

I would just watch. Even if they were doing something they weren't supposed to be doing, I would rarely step in. I would just watch them, and almost always, it would stop. At first, they were very uncomfortable. When I watched them, they thought it meant they should change something about what they were doing. Gradually they got comfortable with me just observing them.

When I looked at them during rehearsal, I got a similar response. Students would look up and see me with a big smile on my face, saying to them, "Keep it up, you're doing great!" and as soon as their eyes met mine, they would be terrified, and duck back under their music stands like prairie dogs. It took them about three months to overcome their fear of being "caught" watching and start to just watch.

I still fight score watching to this day, and your seminar reminded me of that, but I am sure that more than a few directors have had the experience of having their groups afraid to watch them. Eye contact is an important tool of classroom management, and you can do a lot with just your eyes, but it is important to remember that you can dissuade students from watching you if you don't balance the positive with the negative.

What a wonderful example of our ability, through simple human conditioning, to alter behaviors—for the good or the bad. If we stay ever vigilant to guard against the latter, we can focus on making the most of the former. During those all too brief moments rehearsing, we can help shape the positive actions and attitudes of our students. Helping them be what they can be. Encouraging them to become *what we know* they can become. So how can we help condition that positive invisible connection with every performer, one that will allow us to share and communicate all that is wonderful—all that is so glorious—about each of them and our art? How can we strengthen those links that allow for meaningful communication in rehearsals, fostering productive behaviors and outcomes? Let's think about that.

Do we look every ensemble member in the eyes before starting rehearsal? In that way we set the stage of expectations and provide an inviting atmosphere.

Do we take every chance we can to make eye contact with our students *outside* of rehearsal, such as when we pass them in the hallways or cafeteria? What a wonderful opportunity to reinforce that connection as often as possible.

Do we make it a point to look at every student at least once during warm-up exercises? If we glance at every student once before starting and again in the warm up, even one glance to each of them during the rest of the rehearsal will ensure they all leave our room having had at least three reinforcing moments of positive eye contact.

Do we include some warm-up exercises our students can do by memory, allowing us to use that time to foster communication and eye contact? This is the perfect chance to strengthen the bond with students who are still struggling with watching the conductor while reading music.

Do we look toward the sides of the ensemble as much as the front of the ensemble? If we don't, we condition those on the sides not to look up since there is little chance of real communication with us.

Do we look toward the back of the ensemble as much as the front of the ensemble? Sheer distance can make this difficult, depending on the size of the ensemble, but we must be vigilant not to let proximity dictate a student's feelings of importance or the power of his or her connection to the conductor.

Do we make eye contact with our weakest students or do we avoid eye contact with them as we concentrate on communicating with our strongest? Or do we ignore the strongest because they are capable and connect more with the weakest to help them? Again, a student's ability mustn't determine our success in connecting with each of them as human beings.

Do we make eye contact with our performers when things are *good* and *right* as often as when things are *bad* and *wrong*? Identifying errors can overshadow finding excellence. We must work to have *our eyes* catch them doing something well as often as we identify when they do something poorly.

Do we reinforce and reward those students who watch best, so they continue to be great watchers, as much as we work to condition those who never look up so they become great watchers? Often as dedicated teachers we work tirelessly to train our weakest watchers to learn that skill. If we are not careful, however, innocently *ignoring* those who do watch can condition them to *stop* watching, sending the message their eyes are no longer as valued.

Without a doubt, our responses to our students' actions directly and indirectly impact the success of our mutual communication, communication whereby emotions and feelings need not be said, for they are seen from one pair of eyes to another. Through our every word and deed we facilitate and condition the behavior of our ensemble members, and they us. If we provide an inviting atmosphere of shared communication, and reinforce the expectations and virtues of that profound interpersonal contact, we will foster an invisible connection. Though invisible to all, its power and depth are at the very heart of what we teach, and more important, why we teach it. ◼

REHEARSING WITH
PURPOSE

Rehearsals. We sure do a lot of them. But why do we rehearse? I guess the simple answer would be to help our students improve and achieve great results. We all know, however, the far more important answer: we use rehearsals as a vehicle for starting our students on the lifelong journey that is learning, growing, sharing and emoting. Rehearsals are an important platform from which we can invite our students to join us in creating wonderful music that will allow them to rise to heights they never dreamt possible.

I always thought the *purpose* of a rehearsal was to help our students to work hard at getting better, to convince them that great effort would produce great results. That was, at least, until I read the following excerpt from Michele Scherneck's *The 100 Simple Secrets of Successful People*: "Effort is the single most overrated trait in producing success. People rank it as the best predictor of success when in reality it is one of the least significant factors. Effort, by itself, is a terrible predictor of outcomes because inefficient effort is a tremendous source of discouragement, leaving people to conclude that they can never succeed since even expending maximum effort has not produced results."

While reading those words I began to tremble and my heart raced as my educational philosophy was shaken to its very core. Much of what I believed for so long about teaching was brought into correct focus as I thought back to one specific teacher I had many years ago. It all started when I decided I wanted to play golf. I thought it looked like such fun and everyone I knew who played loved the game. So I went to the local golf course and asked about lessons.

After buying my first golf club I was introduced to my teacher. A friendly gentleman, he walked me out to the driving range where he proceeded to teach me how to stand, hold the club, address the ball (you know, where you say, "hello ball!") and swing the club. He patiently taught me those basics and then instructed me to come back that evening and hit a basket of golf balls toward a wooden sign out in the driving range, counting the number of times I hit it. Excited as could be with my new found sport, I dutifully hit all the balls in my basket. Now most of them did go in the direction of the sign, sadly more often than not ending their journey an inch or two from the tee, while the rest ended up somewhere in the parking lot behind me. But one thing's for sure, none hit the sign.

So the next morning I arrived back at the golf course for my second lesson. After welcoming me back and asking me if I had done my basket of homework my teacher asked me how many times I hit the sign. I replied, "None." He shook his head in disbelief as he said, "Peter, you're just not trying hard enough. You need to put more effort into this." He then instructed me to hit a *bushel* of balls that evening with

the same goal of hitting the sign as many times as possible.
So I did. The next morning we replayed the scene from
the day before with me again telling him I failed to hit the
sign even once. He became angry and snarled words to me
about hard work, effort and trying harder, ending with my
new assignment to hit *two* bushels of balls at that sign.

That evening I hit *four* full bushels. I hit so many balls
that my hand bled through my golf glove. By the end I was
at once outraged, demoralized, disappointed, frustrated and
angry, but I was no closer to hitting that sign even once. The
next day my teacher greeted me for our lesson with a cheery,
"So, how many times did you hit it?" I mustered up all my
courage and said, "None." His reply is etched in my mind:
"Peter, I won't teach you anymore. You obviously don't want
to play golf very badly because if you did you would work
harder and put in the effort." My friends, he was the greatest
teacher I ever had, for if his goal was to *teach me* that I could
never play golf, he succeeded. That was thirty-two years
ago and I have never since stepped one foot on a golf course
or ever held that club again. That lesson was taught and,
sadly, learned about as well as it could ever have been.

After reading Scherneck's passage several times, I could
hear myself in those words, asking kids to work harder with
more effort. I then realized more than ever that hard work
and effort, though needed for any accomplishment, could
be counterproductive and discouraging if not correctly
focused, appropriate in nature and targeted in purpose. All
too often we confuse busy with beneficial and active with
achievement, forgetting, as the Roman philosopher Seneca
warned, "When a man does not know what harbor he is
making for, no wind is the right wind."

Or as Stephen A. Covey put it, "Suppose you wanted to arrive at a specific location in central Chicago. A street map of the city would be a great help to you in reaching your destination. But suppose you were given the wrong map. Through a printing error, the map labeled 'Chicago' was actually a map of Detroit. Can you imagine the frustration, the ineffectiveness of trying to reach your destination? ... you could try harder, be more diligent, double your speed. But your efforts would only succeed in getting you to the wrong place faster."

In teaching, as in so much of life, effort is not a technique, hope is not a strategy. Activity does not necessarily yield productivity. So our goal then must be to focus more on rehearsing with *purpose* rather than simply rehearsing with *effort*. Continuing the sailing metaphor, we can heed the advice of Jimmy Dean who stated, "I can't change the direction of the wind but I can adjust my sail to always reach my destination." Though countless books and articles have been written by others far more knowledgeable than I will ever be, what follows are a few thoughts — divided into categories of basic concepts, warm ups and how we rehearse — on making *any* rehearsal more productive.

Basic Concepts

CHARACTERISTIC TONE

As music teachers we have many goals for our students. But of all the important goals we work toward, characteristic tone must number at the top of the list. Certainly every other goal — technical or expressive — is incumbent upon achieving a beautiful, characteristic tone. Until students

can play or sing with a fairly good, characteristic tone quality, time spent working on everything else is like chasing a
moving target. It may be fruitful but is more often frustrating. We may achieve positive results but without the foundation of that timbre those results rarely stick.

Teaching characteristic tone is very important, but
essential at the start is teaching the three precursors to that
success: posture, position and breathing. Without them, all
is for naught.

Posture. I've said it before and I'll say it again: never underestimate the power of posture. We all know it is the foundation of performing, but we get tired of saying things like
"back away from the chair" and "feet flat on the floor" over
and over again. My answer? Don't. Ever. That's right; don't
ever say those phrases again. Saying them is tiring and exas-
perating for the teacher and comes off as nagging to the
students. It's like the old adage about teaching a pig to sing:
"It frustrates you and annoys the pig." So don't say them.

Instead I explain why posture is important in age-appro-
priate terms and then tell them what to do as I reinforce
those attributes of good posture with a representative signal.
So after telling them why their feet flat on the floor and their
backs away from their chairs facilitates correct playing position and breathing, I then say, "Okay, feet flat on the floor,"
as I pound my foot on the floor as a signal for that action.
After making sure each student has complied I say, "Now,
backs away from the chairs," as I slap the small of my back
for that signal. I may do that process once or twice, but after
that, my students will never hear those words again. Instead,
I will simply use the signals they have come to understand.

I then use those shorthand signals to remind those who need reminding whether it is the entire band or a few errant folks. If the clarinet players are slouching in their chairs I walk over to them, stare at them intensely and slap the small of my own back. With that one sound they are instantly reminded; no words, no nagging, no frustration. If trombonists don't have their feet flat on the floor I look at them, calmly say, "trombones," and stamp my foot on the floor. Think about your favorite posture pet peeve, come up with a signal, teach it to your students and then promise yourself you will never say it again. It is so amazingly liberating.

Position. Just as with posture, we know the importance of position to performance. Whether it's left hand position for the violinist, head and neck position for the singer, fingers close to the keys for clarinetists, or fingers rounded on the valve caps for trumpet players, they are all crucial to success. Again, my answer is to teach it once, then train them with the use of silent signals.

A look in the right direction, coupled with my loudly slapping the back of my own left hand shaped as if it's holding an apple, reminds violinists of the task at hand. If I look at the sopranos as I place my hands under both sides of my jaw bone as if to align my head, every singer in the room knows the problem as well as the solution. If I show my left-hand fingers firmly touching the knuckles of my right hand, clarinetists know what to do. And a signal of rounded right-hand fingers with tips touching those of my upward pointing left hand offers all the information needed for those trumpet players suffering from a lapse of memory.

In addition, the use of mnemonic devices or props can be most helpful. For example, using an empty soda bottle to teach flute embouchure or bowing in the channels of an upside-down, empty egg carton held in the left hand to facilitate correct bowing direction. Anything like that can help promote correct habits, develop kinesthetic memory and expedite results.

Breathing. Quite possibly no single topic about performing has created as much controversy or as many techniques as teaching people to *take in air*. I have a pretty simple solution. I don't bother. In fact I never even mention it. That's right; why talk about inhalation? It's too hard to see and feel when it's done well, and way too easy to cheat and do it poorly. I want to teach breathing in a way that is fail-proof, fool-proof and cheat-proof. The answer: exhalation. In a nutshell, I want students to have no choice but to breathe correctly, taking it from a voluntary action they must decide to do well to an involuntary response their body does automatically.

To do that I summon a student's caveman or cavewoman ancestors and their "fight or flight" response. Let me explain. Picture a caveman; we'll call him "Steve." Steve is quite out of shape, so much so that for years his cardiologist has been nagging him to exercise by running. And though Steve's personal trainer has taught him the *correct way* to run, Steve, being a bit lazy and not really seeing the need to exert himself that much, decides not to bother. Then one day Steve is sitting in his camp admiring the stars, when out of nowhere appears a ferocious saber-toothed tiger primed to attack. Steve does not sit there thinking about what to do;

instead his instincts instantly and automatically kick in. He runs like the wind. His actions happen as a panic response to that situation. When a fight or flight instinct comes into play there is no thinking about how to avoid a response or be creatively lazy. Steve has one option: run like his life depends on it, because it does.

That's how I help students "decide" to breathe correctly: I make it so whether or not they *want* to, they know they *have* to. I simply have students sit with beautiful posture and then ask them to blow all of the air out of their lungs with one long, continuous waft of air from the mouth. However I tell them that there are three catches: they must empty every bit of air from their lungs, they cannot take another breath until I tell them to, and when they do breathe they must keep their shoulders down. Then, using an down-ward-and-outward-moving, sweeping motion with my arm to "conduct" the gust of air they are to make, I have them exhale until there is dead silence, all the while reminding them *not* to breathe. I wait just until they seem a bit con-cerned but not long enough for them to get woozy. Then with another, now-fast gesture of the arm back to where it started, I tell them to open their mouths and breathe. The next thing you will hear is the sound of a large group of people breathing deeply, fully and correctly, not because we taught them the muscle system of the torso, lectured about the proper manner to inhale or berated them to do so, but because they thought — no, they instinctively felt — they had no other option.

Basically, here's what happens when I start this exercise. At first my students *think*, "Oh, isn't this a cute little exer-cise the bald man is making us do." Then they *think*, "I don't like this exercise the bald man is making us do." Their next thought: "I don't think I like the bald man!" Then, finally, you know what they are thinking? They're not! At that point their fight or flight mechanisms have kicked in and they are no longer thinking at all. Quite simply, their survival instincts will have taken over all thought and will have told their bodies that at the first chance they better take in air or they will die. And since their lives depend on it, you can bet that fight or flight reaction will ensure the best diaphragmatic breath possible. No thinking, no deciding, no wanting to, just the life-saving response built into every human being.

Certainly we must use care never to risk any chance of ill effects. I would never do this more than twice in one rehearsal. I always have students do it from a seated position, just in case anyone gets lightheaded, and I never have them wait to breathe so long as to worry. And though in 25 years of doing this I have never had a problem, you should seek counsel and permission from administrators before deciding to try it. (There, now with that disclaimer you can't sue me if Bill or Susan fall to the floor after the eighteenth time of doing the exercise or if you wait an hour before letting them breathe!)

The purpose is to train them to always breathe correctly by having them experience it enough that it becomes a kinesthetic memory. Once that takes hold, all we need do is remind them to exhale; the rest is a physical response they will remember. I do this by using a smaller version of that same sweeping arm motion, as a *hand signal*, to "conduct" their exhalation just before I give an initial preparation to begin playing or singing. Early on in the process I do this for every single preparation to truly reinforce the action.

Over time, when it becomes a true habit pattern, the need for that motion disappears. So you see I never did talk about inhaling because to me the key is simply exhaling.

Resistance. The first step is certainly to get students to take in vast quantities of air the correct way. But then all we have is an ensemble of people armed with an enormous amount of air. Frankly, if we don't go to the next step of teaching them *resistance*, how to manage all that air, all we will have done is equip our students with the ability to blast or shout. Probably the best technique for teaching resistance is to have students make a very loud, continuous, intense "hissing" sound after taking a good breath. However, often when this is done, the hissing sound performers make renders the exercise unproductive and worthless, producing a weak, insipid, unfocused hiss more resembling air simply leaking out of their mouths like a leaking tire.

To help students feel the sensation of resistance, after I ask them to make that hissing sound, I have them *crescendo* until it becomes loud, intense and vibrant. While they imitate the sound of a vicious snake, I ask them to feel that their stomachs are firm as they "push" the air out. A few rounds of that, as long as the volume of the "hiss" stays loud, and they will understand the feeling of resistance.

Sustaining that intense sound for longer and longer amounts of time — on one breath — becomes our goal. I do this with a "hissing contest," having students ensemble "hiss" as I count seconds, or for younger students as I use a stopwatch, to time how long they can sustain that sound. Time stops when I see anyone take a breath or the sound starts to fade in volume or intensity. We'll do that a few times until we arrive at our "best time." That number goes on the chalkboard. I repeat this every day, replacing the old record time with the new one. By the third day no explanation is needed; the teacher needs only look at his or her watch or pick up the stopwatch and the signal is sent. The time this activity takes is insignificant; the ability it promotes, inestimable.

However I have always found that once students pick up their instruments and begin to play, because no embouchure imitates hissing, it is difficult for them to transfer that feeling. Often due to the kinesthetic memory developed for their embouchure they just revert back to their old ways. So I "trick" them through this transition from "hiss" to playing embouchure.

I tell them I want the next sound they play or sing, let's say a unison concert A, to be the loudest *forte* they have ever heard. I go on and on about wanting them to make my ears bleed and that they better take in a ton of air to do that. But, I tell them, they must breathe with me, attack with me and listen to me very carefully. Then after using my hand sign to get them to exhale completely I conduct a giant preparatory gesture. However, just as I am ending that gesture, with my hands still in the air, I firmly tell them to only play *piano*. The result will be students taking in the necessary foundation of enormous amounts of air, releasing only a small amount in a most intense, controlled, resistant manner. Though we can only "fool" them like this once in a while, it really works.

Tonguing Through Air. Despite breathing correctly and working for resistance, one of the most common problems

we encounter is the "choppy" sound often created by inex-
perienced performers. Certainly understanding the idea
of shaping melodies and a musical phrase go a long way
toward helping, but often the problem is caused by the way
students relate their tonguing to their air stream. Teaching
tonguing with the use of syllables is a valuable approach;
however sometimes those very syllables cause the breaks
in the air stream which create choppy playing. Picture the
motion of your tongue as you repeat the syllable "ta." Your
tongue can accomplish this with a tiny motion, just barely
interrupting the air stream, or it can do it with a very large,
almost back-and-forth motion which virtually shuts off
the flow of air. In addition it is far too easy for students to
tongue with little or no resistance. As complicated as this
problem can be, the cure is simple and fun.

The first step is to give each child a plastic bar straw and
a flimsy, thin sheet of paper like that from a small (3 ½" × 2
½" is perfect) note pad. Then have the students sit facing to
one side, holding the paper by one end so it hangs down in
front of their faces. Now have them blow through the straw
aimed at the bottom of the paper so the air stream forces
the paper to bend away from them. I first have them do this
working toward producing one long, continuous stream
of air. By watching the papers sailing in the air it is easy to
assess each student's achievement: when a paper returns to
its original hanging position, it is clear that student had to
breathe. In addition, the straw perfectly focuses the aperture
and air stream as it helps reinforce the notion of resistance.

Then we use the straws and paper to help explain that
tonguing should be a slight tapping of the tongue, energiz-
ing the air stream if you will, *during* that same *uninterrupted*

steady flow of air, as opposed to a stopping of the air stream each time the tongue attacks. I demonstrate this by blowing air though the straw in a simple rhythmic pattern, having the air flow through the straw exactly as before — still basically pinning the paper in a horizontal bend — but now with the paper jolting slightly each time I use my tongue. Then I show them how the tongue can stop the air stream by doing the same rhythmic exercise again, this time allowing the paper to return to hanging vertically after each attack, stopping the flow of air as I tongue. Again, by having students face to one side as they try these exercises, assessment becomes easy and clear.

With a simple bar straw and sheet of paper, students are now armed with their own training tool as well as a way of getting immediate feedback. I do have two words of caution. First, bar straws are the only thing that works; coffee stirrers have too small an opening, frustrating students, and soda straws have too big an opening, more than likely leading to the entire ensemble passing out on the music room floor if you use them. Second, do not, I repeat, *do not* tell students they are using "bar" straws. Simply calling them "straws" will suffice. Trust me.

Another way to help reinforce the concept of resistance while playing is to have students go back and forth from playing to "hissing" while rehearsing a piece. For example, have the ensemble play the first two measures of a work as written, then without stopping "hiss" the rhythm of the next two measures, continuing through a portion of the piece alternating back and forth in this way. Or have them play a scale in whole notes, interspersing a measure of "hissing" after each pitch.

Teaching Tone. With the precursors to success established, we can begin the challenge of teaching tone. Teaching characteristic tone, without a doubt, can sometimes
feel as overwhelming a task as describing the color yellow
to someone without sight. Think about it. Describe the
tone quality of your favorite trumpet player. Go ahead, try.
"Well, it's brilliant, warm, majestic and regal." Great, but
that could just as easily be a description of watching the
Queen of England on a hot summer's day! Words just don't
work. Yes, we need to offer helpful descriptors and techniques for achieving that sound, but nothing replaces the
sound itself. And therein lies the rub.

When was the first time you heard a truly remarkable
performer on your instrument or voice part? Junior high
school? High school? College? More often than not, it's
later rather than earlier. If you are a trumpet player, when
was the first time you heard Gilbert Johnson, Adolph Hers-
eth or Philip Smith? Or if you're a clarinetist, the timbre
of Mitchell Lurie, Anthony Gigliotti or Stanley Drucker?
How can we possibly expect our students to describe the
color yellow if they have never seen it? The use of compact
disk recordings as part of some method books has helped
the problem but I believe we can go much further.

We need to have recordings of the best examples of
characteristic tone for every instrument or voice part we
teach. Not passages of technical virtuosity, but reflective
passages of remarkable tone that students can listen to and
absorb. Who better to teach characteristic tone to clarinetists than Maestros Lurie, Gigliotti, Drucker and the like?
As students walk into the music room and get ready for
their clarinet lesson — *trained* to do so in silence — they

hear passages of astoundingly magnificent tone quality. At the end of the lesson, as they pack up and depart, they get another dose of the same. And in the middle of a lesson when timbre is waning, a few seconds from that recording can renew the goal's focus. They hear what they are striving for. They see yellow from the brush of artistic geniuses.

The same holds true for ensemble rehearsals. What better to improve overall ensemble tone quality, balance and blend than to hear recordings of the United States Navy Band, Chicago Symphony Orchestra or Mormon Tabernacle Choir as students enter the room and ready themselves for rehearsal, and as they leave? Will this still allow time for them to warm up? Sure, but let's face it, they don't need a great deal of time for that, and I think we would all rather hear the CSO than the cacophony often heard before rehearsal.

Certainly, teaching all performers they are responsible for their own tone quality, never allowing students to play so soft or loud as to not have a beautiful tone, and including long-tone exercises in our warm ups go a long way toward our goal. In addition we all know how incredibly valuable and important it is to always program compositions—"tone pieces"—with few technical concerns, pieces that demand extreme attention to quality of sound and musicality. But essential to the success of all these efforts is that students be taught to create and control *every part* of *every sound* they make.

I teach that as each sound having a "bloom," which just like a flower includes a beginning, middle and end. A flower pops open, then stands completely exposed and full-bodied before collapsing as it fades. For a sound, those parts become an attack, center or core, and a release. So often students pay greater attention to attacks because they are more obvious, and give little worry to the core and release. In addition, as a result of our concern for rhythmic precision, we frequently attend to attacks more, assuming that if all of the attacks "line up" then the rhythm must be correct. Though there is some truth to that, time spent working on rich, resonant centers and controlled, elegant releases can never be underestimated. Truthfully, I'd rather hear an ensemble perform one profoundly beautiful sound with a focused attack, luxurious core and lingeringly tapered release than four hours of warm-up exercises resembling a horse going through its paces, where more attention is paid to the quantity, rather than the quality, of what is played.

BALANCE

With the incredibly fine "building material" of performers with good characteristic tone, we can build the "foundation" of a balanced sound for the musical "house" that will make possible growth and success in every other aspect of performance. Writings and sessions by the remarkable Dr. W. Francis McBeth have long offered a cogent approach to the teaching of the pyramid of balanced sound. Students can easily understand *where they fit* in this concept of a pyramid of proportionally relative volumes ranging from soprano at the top to bass on the bottom. After they understand that concept for the *entire ensemble*, we can go on to describe how the pyramid must also function—in the same way—within each *family* of instruments and within each *section* of like instruments.

Once we have explained the concept and trained students in our ensembles to produce that balanced sound, I

like to have them hear the alternative: a poorly balanced
sound. And though having them hear the playing of a balanced, then unbalanced chord — side by side — is good, I
think we can go one step better. I start by telling students
that I am a pyramid, or more precisely, my arms are the
sides of a pyramid, as I move both arms diagonally inward
in front of me to represent the sides of a balanced sound.
Next, I change that shape to an unbalanced pyramid with
my arms pointing diagonally up and away from me, out to
the side.

After we perform examples of balanced and unbalanced
chords "correctly," I ask them to start playing and follow
my arms from an unbalanced pyramid, without stopping,
gradually shifting to a balanced pyramid with the correct
changes of volume required. The look on their faces as
the unbalanced sound morphs into a balanced sound is
unforgettable. This exercise seems to have far more impact
than the simple comparing of two separate sounds. I then
explain that my *signal* to remind them of correct balance
will simply be my left hand and lower arm extended diagonally inward in front of me as if to represent the side of a
balanced pyramid. From that moment on, in rehearsal or
concert, students understand my balanced pyramid hand
signal as a subtle — though powerful — reminder to attend
to the concept of a balanced sound.

However, that exercise does far more than compare
balanced and unbalanced sounds. It vividly portrays an
insidious problem often neglected when fixing balance in
rehearsals. Almost always when I practice balance by mor-
phing from unbalanced to balanced sounds, the balance is
corrected but at the expense of the overall dynamic level.

Quite simply, the unbalanced *forte* we start with ends up being a balanced *mezzo piano*. In other words, the top half of the pyramid got softer more than the bottom half got louder. Students must be reminded that an unbalanced *forte* must still be *forte* once balanced. Surely sometimes we would want that balanced sound *with* less overall volume and it will pose no problem, but we need to guard against achieving a balanced sound at the expense of overall dynamic levels when it is not appropriate.

Another commonly heard problem with balance is what I refer to as "dinosaur back." Picture the drawing of a balanced pyramid but with sharply pointed "spikes" coming off each side. This is the sound of an ensemble that is "basically" balanced from soprano to bass but with *sections* that are unbalanced, each spike representing the top of an unbalanced pyramid within our "basically" balanced pyramid. So even though the flutes may be generally balanced relative to the entire ensemble, if the first flutes are louder than the second flutes, their upside-down (unbalanced) pyramid will result in spikes at the top of our ensemble's "balanced" pyramid. Compound this problem with imbalance in every section and you have a pyramid with spikes running from top to bottom. Simple exercises working on section balance as well as judicious assignment of parts within each section (weighting quality and quantity to help create the desired balance) will go a long way toward fixing this problem.

INTONATION

A few pages ago I wrote, "Quite possibly no single topic about performing has created as much controversy or as many techniques as teaching people to *take in air*." Well I was wrong. I think the topic of intonation would give it a run for its money. Intonation: that—sometimes thought of as—elusive, "Holy Grail" of ensemble performance. Working on the concept of intonation, whether in lessons or ensembles, with warm-up exercises or pieces, is like taking vitamins.

Does any one vitamin cure anything? Does any vitamin work instantly? Can you know for sure what vitamin will work best for any one person in a group? Would taking twenty pills of any vitamin, but only once a month, do any good? The answer is surely "no" for all four questions. The best bet is to take a modest dose of a multivitamin every day. In so doing, those regular doses of many different vitamins will offer your body what it needs to be healthy, even though the results may not be obvious.

The same holds true for intonation. No single exercise can be a panacea. No one exercise will be the best prescription for every student. And waiting until the pitch is so bad that we can't stand it anymore, then spending forty minutes on it, will yield little. A variety of techniques and exercises to improve intonation, in many small doses, every day, though very modest in amount of time, will offer the diversity and frequency needed to promote long-lasting results. Diversity: so no exercise becomes routine, and because no one technique will be the best to help every student. Frequency: because *intonation is a habit to be lived, not a problem to be solved.*

Different Pitches. In that different pitches are necessary or better for the tuning of certain instruments, why not use two or three different tuning pitches in each rehearsal and vary which they will be? It prevents tuning from becoming routine, targets the usefulness of the pitch, and promotes the ability to tune to any pitch, not just a single "tuning note."

Find the Pitch. Having students "find" the note on which they wish to tune through a short phrase is an excellent way to have students center the pitch and help them learn to tune horizontally. Tuning on "do" with phrases like, "so-la-ti-do" or "mi-re-do" reinforces the idea that tuning is a musical as well as technical ability. This works especially well as an exercise using a drone on "do" played mechanically, or by other students, to which those playing the moving passage can "arrive."

Set Pitch with Articulation. If an ensemble attack is ragged, it is much more difficult to hear imperfections of intonation. However, when an attack is firm and clean, any discrepancy is far more obvious. Try it: roll the two tones of an octave on a piano so it sounds like a snare drum flam. Then strike the same two tones simultaneously with one clean attack. The intonation of the latter is always easier to judge. The ability to perform clean, precise attacks — like characteristic tone — is a precursor to good intonation.

Tuning from the Bottom. Simply stacking tones, one section at a time from the bottom of an ensemble to the top, fosters the notion of listening down and tuning to the foundation, makes it easier to hear quality of intonation, and reinforces good balance.

Tuning Vertically and Horizontally. The ability for students to tune individual pitches in isolation is necessary. However, equally if not far more important is the ability to tune up-and-down (*vertical*) sonorities, such as intervals and chords, while tuning side-to-side (*horizontal*) pitches moving forward. Sometimes referred to as harmonic and melodic tuning, I refer to them as tuning like a "plus sign," as I make the sign of a giant plus sign with my forearms. Over time every student will learn that tuning vertically, adjusting like partials and chord members, and tuning horizontally, adjusting as one moves linearly from one pitch to the next, are the crux of learning to play in tune. The value of vigilant attention to them and time spent on them, individually and collectively, can not be overestimated.

Rotational Tuning. Much of the time we spend working on intonation in large ensembles has one major flaw: far too many people are playing at any one given time to allow anyone — teacher or student — to hear what's going on. To remedy that problem many use the "let's go down the line one by one" approach to tuning. Though occasionally it can be necessary, the amount of time it takes can make it suspect at best and counterproductive at worst. However, trying to tune *en masse* can be just as fruitless. The solution: rotational tuning.

Many years ago I developed this technique as an expedient way of more or less "going down the line," and it has been my favorite ever since. It is based on the idea of *rotational conducting* which I first encountered in a composition written by my dear friend, Fisher Tull. In the piece, he wrote short, quasi-aleotoric passages that performers were

told to play the moment they saw the tip of the conductor's baton cross in front of their faces. The conductor was
to hold the baton with outstretched arm and arc horizontally from one side of the ensemble to the other, creating a
sweeping radius from conductor to the eyes of every player.

I decided to adapt that wonderful idea to improving
intonation. After I establish which pitch we will be using,
I ask students to play one beautiful tone of about two
seconds in length — with the attack, core and release of a
perfect "bloom" — every time they see the tip of my baton
meet their eyes. When I am ready to start I have an oboe
player sound the pitch, checking it with an electronic tuner.
As soon as the oboist looks at me, signaling he or she is in
tune, I draw my outstretched arm and baton from one side
of the ensemble to the other. I can do this as many times at
whatever frequency and whatever speed I wish.

The virtues are many: *only a few people at a time are playing*, so they can hear themselves; discrepancies in pitch
become extremely obvious; the reference tone from the
oboe can easily be heard; if mallet instruments are part of
the ensemble we will have fixed reference pitches occasionally interspersed in the texture to help stabilize pitch; we
can far more easily assess each player's tone, bloom and
intonation; by sweeping more often in any one area, we can
isolate or focus on any section needing more attention; and
it is as efficient as it is effective.

Try this technique with students playing single tuning
pitches, then with randomly chosen pitches of a specific
interval or chord. Ultimately it can serve as a fast way
to attend to any vertical sonority, be it unison, interval
or chord you are rehearsing in any composition. Simply

announce the spot and as soon as they see the "signal" of your outstretched baton off to one side, they will know what to do.

Isolating Sections. Again, in an effort to improve our ability — and our students' ability — to listen, hear and attend to intonation, I like to have the entire ensemble hold a beautiful, consonant triad. Then I conduct a release for all, except one section which is to continue to sustain.

Chaos to Consonance. Ask students to play any random, very low pitch they like — the more dissonantly chaotic the better. They must, however, play it softly, with beautiful tone quality, and as a continuous long tone with only one attack. It should sound like musical "fog." Then, on cue, they are to move smoothly, without increasing volume or taking a breath, to any member of a given major triad. This exercise seems to force them to assess and act upon their intonation quickly as they arrive at the consonant triad.

Moving Members. This simple exercise helps students isolate, adjust and learn pitch tendencies for each member of a triad by rotating through its pitches. I start by having the ensemble sound a given major triad, each student randomly choosing one of the three pitches. Then, on cue, they all are to move smoothly to a different member of that triad. Another cue takes them to the third of the three pitches before finally returning to the original pitch.

Changing Register. Very often what causes intonation difficulties for students is the register in which a tone or passage is written. To address a passage written in an extended register or simply a bad register for that instrument or voice, one helpful technique is to have students perform the offending tones, chord or passage in their most comfortable register. Having the opportunity to concentrate on their intonation in that most comfortable range, students often find it much easier to stabilize their intonation in the original written register.

Pitch Tendencies. Instrumental music teachers know the pitch tendencies — those discrepancies inherent in the design and manufacture — of their primary instrument. In addition, with experience, we gather bits of information about other instruments. But we can't know them all. We do, however, have to help our students playing every instrument know those tendencies and how to compensate for them. To that end, several excellent books have been written that can serve as a valuable resource. Having one handy when teaching lessons or preparing for a rehearsal can save countless hours of frustration for students and teacher alike.

Bending Pitch. Without question, being able to manipulate pitch is essential to all aspects of intonation. When I first started teaching I would ask students to "bend their pitch" as they held it. Often, they wouldn't. They would just look at me blankly. And I, knowing no better, just thought they were being obstinate, that each of them assumed he or she was the one "in tune" and that everyone else was wrong. Over time I realized very few of them actually thought that way. Most of them just had no idea *how* to bend or adjust the pitch. So when I asked them to raise the pitch, all that went up were their eyebrows! It was then I decided to force the issue.

While holding a given pitch, I ask students to bend it very sharp, then very flat and finally back "in tune" as they follow the direction of my finger as it points up, then down and finally horizontally. In this way, we help every student learn to adjust mechanically and aurally.

Tuners. Electronic tuners, though useful for checking problematic pitches, identifying pitch tendencies on various instruments and establishing a tuning pitch, are often used counterproductively. When students play a tone while looking at the tuner, their eyes usually react, by sight, faster than their ears can react by sound. It is much like seeing lightning before hearing thunder. Doing so, they physically tune the pitch based on what they see faster than by what they hear. Though that can be a quick fix, it does little to help with our real goal of having students audiate pitches, tuning—if you will—in their heads before their mouths and hands.

However, electronic tuners can be a wonderful tool for helping students develop their intonation skills. I suggest having students use them as tutors, helping to assess their intonation after students have had a chance to tune by ear. I ask students to place the tuner on a music stand in front of them and tune to it as usual. Once they feel they are in tune, I ask them to close their eyes and play a different pitch, tuning it only by ear. Then once they think they are in tune they are to open their eyes and see how correct they were with the help of the tuner. Whether tuning the pitches of a scale, chord or random interval, using a tuner in this way can help empower a student with the ability to adjust pitch by ear, rather than simply watching the tuner to *see* if they are in tune.

Singing. When it comes to the concept of intonation, the old adage, "No instrumental ensemble will ever *play* any better than they can *sing*," rings very true. Sometimes, however, getting every student to sing is challenging to say the least. Many of them, depending on their age, maturity and previous training will be very willing; others may be equally obstreperous. Well *I* was pretty defiant about eating my first piece of raw fish, too, and now I'm a sushi addict. What made me less than willing to eat uncooked ocean critters is probably what's keeping those students from singing: fear. And we have to remove that fear, or at least obscure it.

I do that by having students *hum* rather than sing until they become comfortable with the idea. Why hum? Because for those who are self-conscious about opening their mouths to sing, there are no worries; no one can tell who is humming and who is not. I find that most of the time, when those kids realize no one is making faces at them, everyone else is doing it, and the sky has not fallen, they will try it. I always start by humming single pitches we are tuning to, easy pitches that offer the best chance of success. As students get more comfortable I slowly move to humming simple major triads.

Once I am convinced the vast majority of students are humming in a reasonably confident manner, it's time to persuade them to sing. I never *ask* them to sing, or even tell them we're going to sing, I just trick them into doing it. First I ask them to hum a given, very comfortable pitch. Then I ask them to hum louder as I increase the size of my conducting gesture. Three or four times I ask for an even louder and more accentuated sound, having them draw more air each time. Then the last time, the second after they start to hum, in one blast of commotion I say, "Now open your mouth to 'ah'" as I sing the pitch that way.

The only tricks are: not to wait even a second before moving from the hum to the 'ah;' to sing *before* they do; to sing *louder* than they do; and to use an obvious, sweeping conducting motion to cue the event as if making it happen. All of that is meant to obfuscate the moment they begin to sing so they sing before they have a chance to realize what's happening and "decide" not to participate. As you listen to them sing, watch as those most reluctant look around to see they are not the only ones singing as they think to themselves, "Oh darn, I'm singing. How did he *do that?*" That look, almost as much as getting an ensemble to sing, is priceless.

Being careful to have students sing only very accessible single pitches at first, you will see them slowly, gradually develop the confidence to sing harder material which demands more independence. From single sounds to chords and melodic passages, it will come if we are patient and don't rush *their* comfort level. Eventually, one of the best exercises I know is to have students alternate playing and singing short phrases or two-measure passages of a composition; the benefits are immeasurable.

Once ensembles are comfortable singing, the sky's the limit. Have them sing chorales, cadences, problem tuning spots; heck, my favorite thing is to have them sing entire pieces. I can't tell you the number of concerts I've ended with the singing of a march as the encore. Once students "get it" about singing, they really get it.

Warming Up

Without question, those first few minutes of any rehearsal, that portion we often refer to as the "warm up," are precious. Time spent getting students mentally and physically limber, focused and receptive prepares them for the work at hand. It helps them ready their musculature, center their sound and gather their sense of ensemble. However, that time is even more valuable when used for training and teaching concepts; put succinctly, developing ensemble *habits*.

If we use the time to "warm them up," as well as teach ensemble playing concepts which are planned and sequenced from an established curriculum, we foster true musical growth. Here we can develop the technical abilities, listening skills and musical sensibilities needed, not just for the concert program being rehearsed at that time, or any given program, but for lifelong musical literacy. We can prepare new material to be learned as well as practice and review material already learned, all the while offering praise and reinforcing positive behaviors.

In addition, this is the best time to train ensembles to watch — to learn those conducting gestures used by the conductor as a non-verbal language — since much of the material used can be performed without printed music. Freed from the shackles of reading music, they have no other option than to watch, and more important, communicate with, the conductor.

Once these skills and concepts are introduced and learned during the warm up they can be transferred to compositions being worked on during rehearsal. Transfer of training, understanding, conditioning, knowledge and ability then become the underlying momentum for growth and success.

Undoubtedly time spent on warm-up exercises at the beginning of a rehearsal can be extraordinarily beneficial. However, small periods of time judiciously spent on such exercises *throughout* the rehearsal for concepts that seem to be deteriorating, skills they are struggling with, or specific material about to be used in a piece, can be invaluable.

Scales

The very mention of the word "scales" is enough to make most ensembles groan. And of all the warm-up exercises ever used, scales have to be the most common. But sadly they are frequently used in a manner far less conducive to musical growth than possible, often not fulfilling the potential value of their two purposes: helping facility *and* intonation.

Facility. The frequently heard routine of playing scales at the beginning of a rehearsal, where students look and act like zombies as they go through their paces, to me is counterproductive. The problem: it has become routine. They are *able* to "get it" by simply banging down mallets, valves and fingers on *autopilot*. Yes, they are practicing facility. But absent attention to posture, position, tone quality, precision, balance, dynamics, flow, intonation and control, how valuable is it really? It becomes an amusical, mechanical, unfeeling, unthinking activity.

We want to help our students develop facility — that is one of the prime reasons to work on scales — but we must guard against it being at the cost of all else. We need to have ensembles practice scales with great intensity of concentration, focusing on speed and dexterity, but always with precision and an awareness of every aspect of correct and artistic performance.

Intonation. Using scales to improve facility is essential; however, using them as a tool for improving intonation is just as important. Scale exercises are one of the most efficient ways to teach horizontal, or what's sometimes called melodic, tuning. Practicing scales very slowly, with incredible focus on tuning linearly, helps students develop their ability to tune the appropriate interval as they move from one pitch to the next.

Adding a drone on the tonic pitch, played by one section of the ensemble or a mechanical device, allows students to attend to their vertical tuning as well. Done that way, as they move from "mi" to "fa" in a major scale against the drone, they will practice tuning a minor second horizontally, as they practice a major third and perfect fourth vertically. Scales performed in canon are also a wonderful way to practice this skill.

A very important tool for the teaching of intonation and scales is the use of Curwenian hand signs. Known best for their use in the Kodály Method, though devised by the Englishman John Curwen, they are an extraordinarily wonderful way of signaling specific scale degrees and reminding students of individual pitch tendencies for each. Once students are taught that the shape of each hand sign shows the pitch inflection of that scale degree, teachers can use them as a reminder. Teachers can also adjust intonation for specific pitches by moving hand signs in the appropriate direction. Transfer of training allows this to be a fabulous tool for the conductor, as useful in exercises as it is in rehearsing a composition.

HARMONIC MATERIAL

What rehearsal warm up would be complete without some time spent on harmonic material? I think we can all agree playing simple chordal progressions written on the board, or chorale settings from a printed page, offer a wonderful vehicle for work on tone quality, balance, blend, vertical and horizontal tuning, articulation, phrasing, dynamic control, and every nuance of musical performance.

Great worth can be found in a range of exercises as simple as arpeggiating chords of a harmonic progression before playing them in block fashion, to the popular routine best known as the "Remington Exercise." This exercise, the variations of which are too many to mention, has the ensemble start on a major triad, with students assigned to or randomly choosing a pitch. They then move down a half step from whatever pitch they were playing, before returning to their starting pitch. That is repeated, next with two half steps, then three, four and finally five. Though many like to continue further in that manner, I like to stop at that point, so the exercise ends with a dominant-to-tonic cadence.

TECHNIQUE

Whether playing from exercise books, examples written on the board from compositions being performed, or memorized drills, ensembles certainly need to spend time developing the speed, accuracy and facility of their technical skills. Time spent on short technical etudes for band or orchestra, arpeggios, speed exercises and the like indeed will be time well spent.

RHYTHM

Perhaps no other musical concept is as — shall we diplomatically say — "finessed" than rhythm. So often students perform rhythms they "kind of" understand. The problem with that, beyond the obvious lack of correctness, is the knowledge can't transfer to other applications. Though it is time consuming, we must help students to truly understand, not just "approximate," the reading and performing of rhythm.

By isolating rhythmic concepts and systematically, sequentially training students to use them — through the use of chanting, echo clapping, rhythm syllables, counting aloud, rhythm training books, or any other technique — we ensure the success of their understanding that language, now and in the future. The techniques used matter far less than the frequency and consistency of their use.

Crucial to students truly understanding rhythm is a grasp of the concept of *internal subdivision,* what I always refer to as the "fastest common denominator." Without question, no one can play rhythmically well without referencing a subdivision of the pulse which will keep that rhythm precise and stable.

As important as that is to an individual's understanding rhythm, its importance is compounded in ensemble playing. I usually explain it to my students by saying, "At any moment in time, I should be able to draw a hypothetical, vertical line down the score and every rhythm should line up." Though my clapping, a percussionist's tapping, or a mechanical sound chirping that fastest common denominator while the ensemble plays may help performers play with more concern for the rhythmic subdivision, I think we then need to help students move that from an external, audible sound to an internalized concept.

For that I have students chant a rhythm or rhythmic pattern we are working on — whether drawn from performance music or as part of a sequenced approach to rhythmic training — while gently clapping the fastest common denominator of that rhythmic material. So if we were working on performing the syncopated figure of an eighth note followed by a quarter note and an eighth note, they would clap the fastest common denominator of running eighth notes, making certain to align each of their chanted sounds with a clap of their hands. Likewise, a difficult pattern of various permutations of two sixteenth notes and an eighth note can be worked on while clapping the subdivision of running sixteenth notes, again demanding the same precision of sounds aligning with claps.

By doing this exercise, students must manufacture the subdivision rather than simply listen to it from an external source. Then, to help them internalize what they were clapping, I ask them to gradually clap softer and softer as they chant the rhythm or rhythmic pattern until finally they are left chanting with no clapping, now, however, with the subdivision firmly planted in their mind. Whether rhythms or rhythmic patterns are drawn from the music at hand, read as exercises from the board or created by the students, they will come to appreciate the importance of the concept of internal subdivision to their ability to perform with true precision. However we choose to attend to it, a well-developed sense of internal subdivision in an ensemble can often be the difference between a good performance and a great performance.

FLEXIBILITY

Brass players know how extraordinarily valuable practicing lip slurs can be. But we often don't incorporate those exercises into our warm up for fear of boring the rest of the ensemble. No doubt any exercise can serve to help everyone to some degree, but lips slurs certainly are more targeted to aid our brass players. I remember once doing large-interval lip slurs with a concert band, and as those who were playing brass instruments struggled, a clarinet player summed it up by saying, "What's the big deal? I have a button to do that!" Well we all know it's not as easy as that, but would time spent on other exercises benefit those woodwind players more?

To that end, I like to combine various exercises, targeting the specific needs of different sections of the ensemble. It saves time, keeps everyone on task and facilitates the most appropriate activities for our students. For example, have brass players play lip slurs to aid flexibility, while the woodwinds practice rapid chromatic scales to aid facility, simply having the starting and ending pitch of the lip slur match the starting and ending pitch of the chromatic scale. Or have the woodwinds practice long tones or arpeggios while the brass players match those pitches buzzing only on the mouthpiece. The variety of combinations is as great as the results they can help provide.

PROBLEM SPOTS

Creating exercises from problem spots in compositions currently being rehearsed, by isolating the concepts or skills needed, is one of the most efficient ways of combining objectives and saving time. Playing a troublesome rhythm from a piece on each degree of a major scale, or using a particularly difficult run as the basis of a speed exercise, can yield great results.

LISTENING

Ultimately is any skill we teach more important than listening? And though we help our students develop that ability in almost everything we do, perhaps no opportunity is better than taking a few moments to do exercises designed *specifically* to focus on that skill, such as having an ensemble sing or play a chorale by memory, *students keeping their eyes closed,* sensing when and how to move solely by listening. Or, again with eyes closed, have the people at the end of each row play a tuning pitch; then using only their ears, have the pitch pass from person to person down the row as if it were the baton of a relay race. Or repeat the same exercise, now with each student playing one degree of a scale or individual pitches of a well-known folksong instead of a tuning pitch.

No matter the material, *what* we use for these activities is less important than *how* we use them. By doing exercises such as these we help students improve intonation, balance, phrasing and every other performance concept. However, just as important, we *sensitize* them to actively listen in rehearsals — with their ears as well as their minds — for the genius of compositional creativity found in pieces of music.

Then as we help them in rehearsals by pointing out *what* to listen for in a work, they develop the skills of an engaged, intelligent, insightful listener.

WATCHING

Students who possess good listening skills and a developed sense of ensemble are certainly vital to the success of any band, orchestra or chorus. However, equally important is an ensemble's ability to communicate with the conductor, fostering technical precision as well as a unified interpretation. Students who have been trained to watch *and understand* the nonverbal language of their conductor are more engaged in rehearsals, finding information and inspiration with every glance.

I have long held that students must be taught the vocabulary of conducting gestures we use to emulate sound in motion—especially those I refer to as *functional* or technical in nature—using exercises that do not require them to read music. During the warm-up portion of a rehearsal, with the ensemble playing only a single pitch or chord, we can train performers to understand gestures for various releases, articulations, dynamics, cues and the like.

Once learned, those gestures can be transferred to our conducting of any composition, sure in the knowledge our students understand what we are trying to communicate. Looking at every single student before giving the first downbeat of a rehearsal sets an expectation of communication; developing that ability through exercises makes it real. Communication that will be the fuel for the journey we share—every member of an ensemble and its conductor—that is as unexplainable as it is wonderful.

How We Rehearse

Abraham Lincoln once said, "Determine that the thing can and will be done, and then we will find the way." Though I am sure he wasn't talking about a rehearsal, could any advice be more perfect? That's *what* we do. We find a way. We take a group from where they are — no matter where that is — and help them grow. Despite any frustration or obstacle we *make real* those words of Albert Einstein from *The Three Rules of Work*: "Out of clutter, find simplicity. From discord, find harmony. In the middle of difficulty, lies opportunity." With planning, preparation, patience, perseverance and a sense of purpose we find a way to help students learn the precision, beauty and growth that is at the core of simplicity, harmony and opportunity. We seize every opportunity to help our ensembles find the wonder and awesome power of music that awaits them.

But we also know, as David Niven warns, "Some problems can be avoided more easily than they can be eliminated, and some solutions are more costly than the problems they solve." Spending fifteen minutes tuning clarinet players may yield some improvement; but if it is at the cost of the rest of the ensemble growing weary, causing some to become discipline problems, was it worth it? Insisting on a volume one level softer than the group can play well may best fit our interpretation, but if it comes at the expense of good characteristic tone, balance and intonation, does it cause more problems than it's worth? Rehearsing one section of a work so much that it sparkles is terrific, only if that use of time doesn't result in the rest of the work being neglected.

So choosing *what we work on* and *how we work on it* is very important to the success of a rehearsal. We must make certain we keep an appropriate pace, spend as much time reinforcing progress as pointing out errors, don't cause problems with our solutions, guard against the routine of always starting at the beginning of a work, and ensure we use our time as effectively and efficiently as possible. Often, though, it is less *what* we choose to spend time on in rehearsals than *when* we choose to spend it. Five minutes of work refining and polishing the contour of a phrase is as absolutely appropriate *at one point* in the course of learning a work as it is futile and inappropriate at *another* point.

ROUGHING-IN

Once a builder has constructed a firm foundation, he or she begins to "rough-in" the structure. This is where the girders, beams and studs are put up to support the building. Nothing pretty. No finesse; just basic, solid, secure construction to serve as the framework for all that follows. Not always starting from front door to back door, or left to right, carpenters work on what makes sense at the time in an order that is logical. They are confident in the knowledge that as long as there is a solid foundation to begin with, the correctness of that roughing-in will make possible every other aspect of the building, no matter how elegant the detail or delicate the filigree.

Trade the hammer for a baton, and doesn't that sound just like us? We know that as long as the previously discussed basic concepts of performance are in place as our foundation, we can rough-in the composition with the same assurance. With purposeful conviction we can start by

attending to those basic "building blocks" of correct notes
and rhythms. Though that may often seem a daunting and
overwhelming task, if we simply isolate rhythm errors by
rehearsing horizontal layers of the same material and wrong
pitches by stacking vertical sonorities from bottom to top,
we can find and correct those "needles" in any haystack.

With those building blocks in place we can continuing
to rough-in the performance of the piece in various ways
depending on the work at hand. We can ensure correct
internal subdivision by working through rhythmically intri-
cate passages slowly like gears fitting together in a clock.
We can practice technically difficult runs by working from
a very firm and slow speed to a fast and confident one.
We can rehearse like horizontal layers of a composition
to ensure precision and independence. Or we can isolate
"events" — those usually short, specific spots with great
density of musical or technical activity — to coordinate
their accuracy. And just like the builder, whether working
from the end of the piece to the beginning, the beginning
to the end, or specific sections later to be linked, we choose
the best path toward success for our students.

POLISHING

With an ensemble now in control of the basic elements of
the piece, we can begin the process of polishing the performance. This stimulating, enjoyable and artistic work is
where we attend to our list of fine points, details, particulars
and subtleties in an effort to refine, clarify and focus them.
Though here we rehearse with great specificity, often focusing on very small details, we must never underestimate the
value of putting what has been rehearsed back into context,

playing those spots as part of longer passages as well as the entire composition.

Contrast, Clarity and Precision

Shades of Gray. Though some music is striking by its conspicuous lack of contrast of musical elements, much music is brought to life through vivid contrasts. All too often, performances of the latter seem as though they are being portrayed with a palate of only shades of the color gray. Yes, contrasts do range from deep, dark gray to wispy, light gray, but never more vibrant than that.

When describing intensity of contrast to an ensemble, I use the wonderful advice of Tom Stacey, who said, "You have to overdo musical effects to get them across to listeners, just as actors overdo makeup for the stage." I ask students to think of classmates they have seen appear on stage in a school musical or play who have beautiful eyes. I go on to ask if they have ever seen those classmates before they went on stage, slathered with so much makeup that up close they more closely resemble "Happy the Clown" than themselves. Makeup so overdone as to be oddly comical. Why? So that when they appear on stage, with the footlights shining brightly, their naturally beautiful eyes are seen by the audience. What may appear overdone on stage is exactly what is needed to carry that quality into the hall.

The same is true for an ensemble. A *subito piano*, *sforzando* or *diminuendo* performed so it sounds good from inside the group will rarely have enough contrast to sound that way to the audience. When appropriate, extremes of contrast may be as useful as those that are subtle. It's not, however, always a case of using *more* to achieve those contrasts.

Indeed I believe we must ask performers to use their *brains* as much as their *muscles* to achieve some contrasts; for example, making what comes before a *subito forte* softer, as much as making the *subito forte* itself louder, or using subtle phrasing before a crushing *sforzando* to give the illusion of even more attack than what's used. It's not a matter of always using a palate of colors from fluorescent purple to neon green, but using them when no shade of gray will do.

Homogenization. Homogenization is great when we're talking about processing milk, and some musical passages, but very often it is a source of imprecision leading to a vagueness of detail. At times we want a unified, cohesive, sounding-as-one, homogenized sound, but at other times we want a sound portraying many distinct facets. It may be we spend so much time — and rightly so — trying to get young musicians to play with a homogenized ensemble sound that when they get older it's difficult to get them to be individualistic, bold and courageous enough to part from the path of unity.

For example, all too often when a measure of ensemble music calls for three distinctly different polydynamic effects, players homogenize them into one quasi-correct sound. So a *crescendo* over the second and third beats of a measure, a *crescendo* over only the first two beats, and a *crescendo* on only the last beat, written simultaneously in three different voices, becomes homogenized, or blended into one *crescendo* of more or less four beats. Would that performance be vile? No, but it would be far from precise.

Whether it's a specific timbre needing to come out of an otherwise unified texture, phrasing that is intentionally different, or varied articulation that needs to be brought vividly to life, attending to what is diverse and distinctive is often vitally important to the success of a performance.

Consonant Mistakes. It would be great if all performance errors sounded as obvious and unmistakable as a minor second. Sadly, they don't. But the most difficult errors to hear in rehearsal are those that sound correct and plausible: what I call *consonant mistakes*. Things we can easily miss because they sound as if they fit, such as solo versus soli, muted versus unmuted, or yarn mallet versus plastic mallet. All of those errors would sound fine, though incorrect.

Fatigue Factor. Sometimes the source of imprecise playing is simple fatigue. It's not that our trombonists can't play a measure of a rapidly-tongued rhythm, it's that they can't play that measure *twelve times in a row* without it sounding as though it has degraded to musical mush. Often the solution is "platooning" (a term which comes from sports), divvying up such passages between those playing them. Though sometimes composers will judiciously do this for us, more often than not we will need to make those decisions. Then, by simply teaching students the term and concept as well as the trick of marking their initials on the part wherever they are to start playing, we can provide an antidote to the inevitable fatigue that often makes such material sound tired and sloppy.

Goal Orientation. So often what makes a performance sound sterile or boring is the lack of goal orientation. From its smallest manifestation of showing the direction, flow and contour of a motive or phrase, to the grand scale of portraying the architecture of climaxes and repose within the overall form of a symphony, an understanding of goal orientation brings a piece to life. Helping our students, through our words and conducting, to shape a line or build to a climax reveals to them this most essential skill. As well, if long lines of continuous material are broken down into smaller sections by identifying goal tones that act as punctuation within the long line, it can be much more manageable and much less overwhelming for performers.

Momentum. I remember learning rules in physics class about an object in motion staying in motion unless acted upon by another force. They made sense and I'm glad I learned them. But far more important to me now are those rules as they relate to what is often heard in ensemble performances, specifically the concept of momentum and how it affects the way young people perform.

In general, relatively slow music, I fear, often suffers from a lack of momentum created by a tempo just a bit slower than would foster a forward flow of musical energy, bogging the performance down and dragging it ever slower and more plodding. Conversely, relatively fast music is often performed at a tempo just a bit faster than can be truly controlled, allowing momentum to drive the tempo faster and faster, sometimes to speeds barely controllable.

Unchecked, those problems can lead us down a path which is as unmusical as it is frightening. In addition, those problems can be exacerbated by the way disparate levels of performers react to technical issues. For example, we have all heard rapid sixteenth-note passages rush from uncontrolled momentum in the hands of technically proficient players, but the same passages slow like the drag of gravity from a lack of facility by weak performers. Likewise, how often have we heard a slow passage of whole notes rush when played by some students because of their perception of how "easy" it is, or the same passage played with gradual slowing from a lack of momentum?

Now picture different aspects of all those problems in the same performance, with momentum pushing the pace forward by some students, drag from a lack of momentum pulling the tempo back by others, and technical proficiency — or the lack thereof — impacting tempo in every direction. It can be a challenging rehearsal dilemma, but a variety of solutions can help with various aspects of the problem.

Sometimes simply taking "slow" music a touch faster and "fast" music a bit slower can make for a more satisfying, comfortable, stable and musical performance. Possibly works of a very slow tempo would be better suited to being performed with a subdivided pulse or faster pieces may benefit from being executed in a hypermeter to better harness momentum. Maybe what's needed is simply more training and drill for dexterity and facility or more grounding in the concept of internal subdivision training discussed earlier in this chapter. But more often than not, the remedy will be an awareness of, and proficiency in, a combination of all of these factors.

Seams. Have you ever spent an enormous amount of rehearsal time on a section of music, a section full of problems? And then, the night of the concert, though that section is played beautifully, the seam or transition *into it* and

from it becomes the problem? I have, and each time it serves
as a reminder to attend better to the seams where two sections join, or transitions where one section evolves into
another. A musical seam, like the seam where two pieces of
cloth are joined, must be secure and firm. A transition, like
when two pieces of cloth are interwoven, must be smooth
and seamless. Either way, they can be as magnificent as they
can be treacherous.

Mud in the Middle. Listen; can you hear it? A performance where the soprano parts, often playing the melody,
are played perfectly; the bass line is stable and solid; but
the middle voices tend to sound murky or less than defined.
This can reveal itself as blurred passing tones, sloppy coun-
termelodies, ambiguous accompaniments, or active rhythmic figures that are less than accurate. It pervades the entire
texture, making everything sound out of focus.

It results from students playing so insincerely, impre-
cisely or inaccurately as to create what sounds like a dull
scrim of cloudy background noise. I liken it to a tile floor
where correct tones are the tiles and this insidious blur is
grout that doesn't just glue the tiles together but covers the
tiles themselves.

Getting students to play with conviction goes a long
way to fixing this problem. We must reward accuracy in
those parts which are more obscure by reinforcing positive
behaviors as well as take every opportunity to highlight
the beauty provided by somewhat hidden treasures, such
as passing tones and accompanying figures. I also think the
way we typically set up an ensemble, while not causing this,
can contribute to it. Think of where that mud comes from;

often the amount increases the farther away from the conductor the sound emanates. I know this a gross generalization, but it is also fairly common.

Think about it: for a modestly motivated player in the back of an ensemble, even the efforts of an animated conductor could be forty feet away, hardly as "in their face" as for those seated in the first row. I fear that sometimes the power of our intensity, no matter how strong, does become more subdued the farther it carries. So on occasion let's equalize that distance. Placing three or four aisles in the setup, each radiating through the ensemble from the podium like a radius, allows us to *take our intensity and conviction to every student*. In addition, those aisles allow us to better assess every student's posture, position, tone, blend and articulation, reinforcing positive behaviors with every step. It is amazing how even a few minutes of using those aisles brings about great improvement.

Or try setting up the ensemble in concentric circles or squares with you in the center. Or allow students to "scatter" themselves in a setup, sitting in random spots, next to different instruments. Again, this allows you to bring your power of personality, your intense attention to precision, your resolve and sense of purpose closer to every student. Each of these techniques, in addition to being fun and creating variety in rehearsals, helps students develop musical independence as well as listening skills.

Breathing as Villain. Though breathing, for most if not all musicians, is the wellspring from which all else comes, it can also cause many problems. These problems include the most basic "taking a breath after every few notes" syndrome, remedied by work on correct breathing and resistance; students breathing on short duration rests before rhythmically active passages, causing the first sound after the rest to be "late;" intentional *luftpausen* or "air spaces" not performed in a unified and secure manner because students have not been trained to write in phrase marks; unwanted breaths that occur because ensembles have not been taught to stagger-breathe or use "no breath" marks; or when the conductor has not remedied the often conflicting problems caused when forces that need to breathe—like winds and voices—perform with those that do not—like percussion, piano and strings.

We can usually resolve these, and the myriad other ensemble problems caused by breathing, by making students aware of the problems and offering simple solutions like having them mark when and where they must or can't breathe and teaching not to breathe on some very short rests.

Delicate Attacks. A most frustrating sound is that of an ensemble afraid to play a quiet, subtle initial attack. The result is what I call a "ruffled" attack: the sound of fifty performers each attacking milliseconds apart creating one long attack that sounds like the musical equivalent of people doing the wave in a football stadium. In that we technically only hear one sound, despite the numerous attacks, it is seemingly innocuous. However, accepting this insidiously sloppy attack, in addition to the obvious imprecision, fosters an ensemble attitude of "well, it's good enough." Encouraging students to over-accentuate those delicate attacks would improve the sloppiness but at the expense of all elegance.

I ask performers to correct the ruffle, that sound of many people lacking as much courage as precision, by "pointing" the sound. I liken it to ballet dancers about to lift themselves straight up in the air by standing on the toes of one foot. To do this, they *point* their foot, firmly placing the downward pointing toes of that foot into the floor with one definite, resolute motion as they lock their ankle to maintain that position. If they were to stamp that foot flat on the floor instead, there would be no possibility of lifting upward. Standing on tiptoes without pointing the toes will result in a broken ankle. Success can be found only in the subtle, though secure, pointing of the toes.

Ensembles must learn that though we appreciate their concern for grace, the lack of precision of the ruffle is unacceptable. And that the thud of a "flatfooted" over-accentuation, though clean, is equally unacceptable. The solution lies in an intensely firm, though rounded and blunt, pointed attack. As I describe these sounds to students, I use my foot to hit the podium. When they hear the difference between a flatfooted stamp and the finesse of a pointed attack of the toe, the concept is brought to life. From that moment on, all I need do is tap the toes of one foot on the podium and everyone knows what needs to be done.

Another source of less-than-precise playing comes when a slurred passage includes a large leap. Can't you just hear a dozen trumpet players slithering to the top of a slur such as that with imprecision, each arriving at the higher pitch at different times? A tiny, almost imperceptible amount of *legato* tonguing on that pitch will provide clarity of movement. That bit of "tongue behind slurs" such as those will offer a wonderful musical compromise, with little downside risk, if done judiciously.

Subtleties of Volume. Often, ensemble problems are caused by one element or aspect of performance negatively impacting another. Though all elements are susceptible to this *negative interaction* of concepts, volume certainly comes into play quite often; for example, a gradual ensemble *crescendo* that begins well balanced, but goes ever more out of balance as it gets louder, or the equivalent, with a decrescendo. Or not compensating for volume when moving from one pitch to several, such as when a unison played by eighteen clarinet players moves to a triad, each pitch now being played by far fewer. If that unison isn't played softer, or the triad isn't played louder, the volume will be heard to decrease when they move, or the opposite when moving from several pitches to a unison.

Another example would be not compensating for changes in tessitura in a passage that should stay the same volume. If we don't guard against it, all too often performers will *crescendo* as they ascend and *decrescendo* as they descend. Couple that with how we perceive higher versus lower frequencies and the problem becomes compounded. We need only make students aware of this tendency and teach them to counteract it.

Interactions of intonation and volume impact every sound an ensemble makes, the clearest example being an unbalanced chord always sounding less "in tune" than one which is balanced. However, one of the most glaringly obvious and often troublesome examples of this is with the playing of octaves. If only I had a dollar for every time

I rehearsed a piece that sounded great *until*, that is, a section where the melody was played simultaneously in three octaves. Octaves: I think there should be a law against them! It's not that they are more "out of tune" than anything else, it's just easier for us to hear how out of tune they are.

Though a change in volume can't *cure* this problem, it can certainly improve how we perceive intonation. I love demonstrating this to students by walking over to a piano and playing an octave—always trying to find one that is poorly tuned. I play the upper pitch far louder than the lower pitch and ask the students to arrive at a number from one to a hundred to represent the quality of intonation. Then I play the same octave again, now with the lower pitch played far louder than the higher pitch. Again, I ask for them to arrive at a number. The second playing always amazes them. And when they realize I can't affect the pitch of the piano when playing it, they become believers: when lower octaves are played louder than higher octaves, intonation is perceived to be better. It doesn't beat a law against the use of octaves, but surely helps.

Conclusion

Conducting a rehearsal is much like being an air traffic controller. Think about it: air traffic controllers coordinate the actions of dozens of pilots each doing slightly different activities. They must possess a true knowledge of what each pilot and aircraft can do and when they can do it; they must weigh the ramifications of every command they give; they know staying calm is always better than flying off the handle (forgive the pun); they worry as much about the psyche of the pilots as the skill of those pilots; and they must choose the *best* course for every pilot they are entrusted to help. Isn't that us?

Rehearsing an ensemble is much like that, juggling a thousand balls in the air at once. It can be overwhelming in complexity but no more so than it is in importance. However, it basically boils down to three things: *when, what* and *how.*

WHEN

Good rehearsals, like good health, require habits and techniques that foster a long, happy and successful journey. Regular doses of what is most beneficial, which continue over the long haul, provide results that are sometimes hard to see at the time. And though what is required and appropriate changes with every age, *it is never too early* to start developing those skills.

In the words of Lao-Tzu, "Begin difficult things when they are easy. Do great things when they are small. The difficult things of the world must once have been easy. The great things must once have been small. A thousand mile journey begins with one step." It is never too early to start that journey, with the smallest of steps; small steps which over time grow to be as priceless as those who take them.

WHAT

When it comes to *what* we rehearse, if progress eludes us, we must remember *it's not them, it's us.* We try our hardest to set the best course, but when that doesn't work, we have to be willing to go back to the drawing board and use our instincts, knowledge and talent to find a better way.

"Knowledge is knowing facts. Wisdom is knowing what to do with the facts you know."

We must sometimes reverse or change course, backtrack, or experiment with different ways. Ways that will perhaps *end up* being better. Ultimately we can't blame our students; the responsibility for their success falls squarely with us. It may be well for each of us to remember the wonderful, truly appropriate Polish proverb that states, "The man who can't dance thinks the band is no good."

We must also possess the vision to see the forest through the trees, the knowledge that the best way to do something may still need to be invented, and the confidence and courage of our conviction. In the words of Edward de Bono, "Removing the faults in a stagecoach may produce a perfect stagecoach, but it is unlikely to produce the first motorcar."

HOW

All this is fine, but to me passion and enthusiasm are the *sine qua non* of rehearsals. Knowing diverse teaching techniques is great. Correctly understanding how to sequence material is wonderful. Preparing a score to the nth degree is terrific. But all that, and just about everything else, is for naught if we lack passion and enthusiasm for what we do. "Life is not measured by the number of breaths we take, but by the moments that take our breath away." Maybe Henry David Thoreau said it best: "Nothing great was ever achieved without enthusiasm."

But what we rehearse *for* — what we *truly* rehearse for — can't be described, discussed or documented. It can't be found in correct rhythms or balance, astounding intonation or characteristic tone. What we truly rehearse for is simply a byproduct of those abilities, for as Antoine de Saint-Exupéry wrote, "It is only with the heart that one can see rightly; what is essential is invisible to the eye." A sentiment made as clear as it is succinct in the words of Igor Stravinsky: "I haven't understood a bar of music in my life, but I have felt it."

After all this, what *really* is a rehearsal? Well I think each one is an opportunity; a new opportunity to help our students along the path of our dreams for their success. An *opportunity* to think about the *quality* of what we do more than the *quantity* of time we spend doing it, aware "it's not the hours you put in, it's what you put in the hours." An *opportunity* to *inspire* as much as *teach*, knowing "you can let things happen or you can make them happen." An *opportunity* to help make an ensemble far more valuable than just the sum of its parts, living those astounding words of Henry Ford: "Coming together is a beginning; keeping together is progress; working together is success."

So I guess when all is said and done, the *purpose of rehearsing* is quite simply *rehearsing with purpose.* ▓

"How Do You Know?"

"There once was an old farmer who kept horses. One night, during a great storm, a section of his fence collapsed, and all eight of his horses escaped. The following morning, several members of the surrounding village came to offer their condolences. The old man asked, 'Why are you so sad?' and the villagers replied, 'You have lost all of your horses: this is a disaster!' To this the old man asked, 'How do you know?' The villagers walked away, shaking their heads in confusion.

"The next day, all eight horses returned, bringing with them twelve wild stallions. The villagers returned, exclaiming their joy for the old man's great fortune. The old man simply asked, 'Why are you so happy?' 'All of your horses have returned, and you now have many more! This is a good thing!' exclaimed the villagers. The old man again asked, 'How do you know?' and again the villagers left, dumbfounded.

"The following morning, the old man's son arose, and went out to tame the new, wild stallions. In so doing, he was thrown, his leg broken. The villagers returned, with great sadness on their faces. The old man immediately

noticed this, and asked, 'What saddens you so?' The villagers replied, 'Your son has broken his leg! This is terrible!'
Again the old man asked, 'How do you know?'

"Not two weeks had passed before the Emperor's men
rode into the village. The war had greatly ravaged their
front lines, and they sought fresh young blood to serve
in their army. The old man's son, however, could not
be drafted, for he had a broken leg. When the villagers
heard about this, they said, 'How lucky! If he had been
drafted he would almost certainly have died or suffered
terrible injury.' The old man said, 'Is it lucky? How do you
know?'"

Does that mean some good things can't be just plain old
good, and it may be virtually impossible to find the good in
some bad that befalls us? Sure. But that remarkable parable
from Lao-Tzu, the father of Taoism, shows us how *our perspective* tempers our view of all that happens to us. *We decide*
how we will characterize all we encounter. I know that may
sound like optimism run amuck, but it's really more about
being a realist.

Things are what they are. The situation I am in *is* the
situation I am in. How am I going to perceive it, what can
I learn from it, how can I grow from it, and what positive
aspect or benefit can come from it? How's that for easier
said than done? But what a wonderful gift we give our students when we help them to understand its truth; what a
wonderful gift we give ourselves when we realize its power.

Picture the two of us sitting in a fancy restaurant having
a cup of coffee after dinner. All of a sudden, I knock my cup
off the table sending the fragile china vessel plummeting
down to the floor. It shatters into a million pieces with a

most violent crash. At that moment, as I sit there horrified and embarrassed, every single patron in the restaurant turns and looks at me. My first thought: "I can't believe all these people are staring at me thinking I am an idiot. They all just *had* to superciliously look at the moron who dropped his cup." I feel so bad.

But *I* am the one who decided to characterize those events that way. The reality of that scenario more likely was that those people suddenly turned and stared at me because they were startled by the loud crash. And human nature being what it is, they simply turned in my direction as a reaction. That's it — nothing more — nothing less. All of those bad feelings were manifested only in my imagination. The reality — the truth — was far simpler. It's all about perspective; how we see our reality, like George Carlin wrote, "Why is it the other side of the street always crosses the street when I do?" It's all in how we see it.

As well, can we always know what good lies in that which we view as bad? And will we necessarily ever be aware of *that good*? Perhaps not, but those virtues, like the ones that follow, may be hiding in the most unlikely places. Each is an opportunity for us to be the best teacher we can be.

Finding Strength

Devastating cuts are being proposed for the music department of your school. You are being called to meeting after meeting with administrators and are having to defend the value of music in education.

As a result, the parents of children involved in music have become motivated and mobilized to fight for what is

right. And possibly even more important, it has strength-
ened your resolve to understand the value of what you do,
commit to being an even more effective teacher, and cherish
every opportunity to teach music to young people. Sometimes we find strength — inner and outer strength — in
places where we would never think to look.

Growth Isn't Always a Climb Straight Up the Mountain

Steve, your best trumpet player, a joy in every way, comes
to you to find out the results of his all-state band audition.
You have to tell him that he didn't make it despite the fact
that he worked harder than he knew possible.

You seize the opportunity to explain how he must keep
that one event in perspective, the reality of auditions, that
no audition result can undermine his hard work and growth,
and that sometimes the falls of life give us the motivation to
climb even higher. Your encouragement at that moment
helps him deal with that news, and with all the disappoint-
ments in his life, giving him the willingness to try harder
after each of them.

Teaching Tools That Last a Lifetime

Susan, a delightful young singer in your choir, could not
remember the names of the notes on a staff. She tried but
failed. She almost quit because she thought she couldn't do
it. You, her teacher, recognizing the problem, call her in for
help and explain the use of the simple mnemonic device,
"Every Good Boy Does Fine."

Years later, fearing she would never pass a chemistry exam on the periodic table of elements, she remembered you and that staff. She passed the exam with flying colors, and once again *you* proved to her that she could learn anything. She still has a burning desire to ask you "every good boy does *what* fine?" and to thank you for what you meant in her life.

Deal with Emotions

While rehearsing a magnificent piece with your high school orchestra, you pause to describe to the students how this emotional work was written in honor of the composer's father who had recently died. You ask them to pour their hearts into each note. You talk about the sadness of losing a loved one and the grief this piece captures. Hard lessons, but lessons that need be taught. For the rest of the rehearsal you notice that Sarah, one of your violinists, is extremely overcome with tears. You quietly walk over and ask if she is okay. She nods for you to continue.

At the end of rehearsal you meet with her. Through the tears she proceeds to tell you that her father was just diagnosed with a disease that will soon take his life. You feel awful that you unknowingly put this child in a state of inconsolable emotional turmoil right there in what should be the safety of your rehearsal.

Months later, only days after her father's passing, Sarah comes to you. She thanks you for your concern and care, but far more significant, she thanks you for helping her learn how music can soothe the heart; how it can make the tears come and then dry them; and how it can offer a way of expressing her sorrow as well as the love she had for her father. She continues describing how that rehearsal, all those months ago, as overwhelming as it was, helped prepare her for the future.

Bolster Self-Esteem

Every day, Bill would come to band rehearsal. Every day, he would hold a clarinet. Every day, he barely would get through rehearsal. Every day, you would grow more and more frustrated at his lack of ability. Without a doubt, he was the weakest link in the chain that was your ensemble. He was the anchor that weighed everyone down.

One day he came to you and said, "I know I'm the worst player in the band, I should just quit. I stink." You found yourself in quite the bad situation. And though fleetingly you thought that might be the best thing for the ensemble, you knew it wasn't what was best for him. As surely as you wondered whether Bill would ever play all that well, you knew he needed band in his life.

You had a long talk with Bill. You took the time to bolster his self-esteem, to convince him you valued his worth as a person just as much as his worth as a performer, that every member contributes to the whole, and that as long as he worked as hard as he could, you would never give up on him.

Twenty years later, a young Bill, Jr. came home from school and asked his dad whether he should sign up to play an instrument. The answer was a resounding "yes" as the dad regaled the boy with stories of his own band rehearsals. But what Bill, Sr. really was remembering was how special and important you made him feel at a time when he didn't feel very important. The fatherly support of his son's music-making was as much about how you taught "the person" that was Bill as about how you taught "the performer" that was Bill, and about the self-esteem you helped instill that has sustained him all his life.

A New Way of Thinking

Joan had been playing the flute for two years, and though she had wonderful posture, perfect hand position, a delightful tone, and dedication that was infectious, she also had no understanding of rhythm. She just couldn't get it. You tried and tried but to no avail. Failure was at hand. She was ready to give up, and so were you.

But you didn't. Instead you started asking Joan's other teachers and guidance counselor if she was having difficulties in other subjects. Slowly a pattern emerged, until finally you realized she was having trouble processing any written material. You facilitated her getting help for a previously undiagnosed special need. Now, with the aid of professionals in that area, she was being helped to find new ways of learning that would work for her. Her life now had possibilities she never imagined.

A New Way of Being

Fred was your star alto saxophonist. He had made it into all-state band since he was a sophomore in high school. He was an amazing player. He also had an amazing ego. At every turn he would remind all around him of just how good he was. Over the years you tried to keep him "in check" through every way possible, using every behavior modification trick in the book, but one night the problem became critical.

At a dress rehearsal for a performance, rehearsing a piece with an extended alto saxophone solo, he finally went too far. He was goofing around, making fun of others and playing in a manner best described as contemptible. After several attempts to right the situation, you calmly asked the second chair player to perform the solo. He did, and though acceptable, it was not anywhere as fine as if Fred had played it. Fred was outraged and he let you know it. You watched as he seethed with anger.

You called Fred in for a meeting. He would barely look at you, let alone speak to you. Finally he blurted out how angry he was that you humiliated him in front of the band, took away his solo, and gave it to someone who couldn't play it as well as he could. You quietly told him that you thought he was a wonderful musician, with a talent that was rare, and you knew he could go on to shine in the future. But you then addressed his comments and said, "Fred, let me correct you: *you* humiliated yourself, *you* lost the privilege of playing that solo, and *the music* and *the ensemble* were better served by a soloist who truly cared more about the joy of making music and less about being a star." You basically let him know his priorities were at fault, and until they changed he would never be the musician he could grow to be.

That "kick in the seat of the pants" served as the "wake-up call" Fred needed. Though a tough experience for a young person to deal with, it was the lesson he needed to change his way of being. For Fred, over time, it became more about the music and less about his ego; more about contributing to the whole and helping others in the ensemble than being the center of attention. The humility he gained from the experience helped shape the person as much as the player.

Conclusion

Do our "bad" situations always turn out that rosy? Can we be sure those benefits appear even though they may arrive years after students leave our lives? Can "bad" situations turn even worse? Do our best efforts sometimes fail? The answers are obvious. But we are teachers, and we know the lessons learned in adversity can sometimes be the most powerful and life-changing of all. May the good in life follow you and your students closely. But when the bad comes, may you help those whom you teach to find growth, change and good in its wake. ▰

"FAR BETTER IT IS TO DARE MIGHTY THINGS..."

"Far better it is to dare mighty things, to win glorious triumphs even though checkered by failure, than to rank with those timid spirits who neither enjoy nor suffer much because they live in the gray twilight that knows neither victory nor defeat." Every time I think of those words of former President Theodore Roosevelt, I am almost paralyzed by their profound power. To me they are the perfect description of a music teacher. Isn't the essence of what we do every day to "dare mighty things" for each of our students?

It doesn't matter whether we are rehearsing a high school orchestra toward the performance of a difficult work, teaching the first steps of learning an instrument to fourth graders, or working on the singing of a round in a second grade general music class. We teach our students to dare mighty things in each of those settings. However, it is the teaching of that very life lesson which is most important. By our teaching we help them to learn to dare mighty things of themselves now, and to continue to do so for all the days of their lives, in every aspect of life. Basically, we teach them to dream big dreams.

But how can we teach them to dream big? Well I believe it happens in three steps. First we dream for them. Then we inspire them to start dreaming for themselves, helping them discover that *what is possible* only comes from *dreaming*. Finally we get them not just to dream, but to dare mighty dreams: to take risks for dreams that are worthwhile, knowing failure may be the short-term price we pay.

Dream for Them

To borrow a sentiment Mark Twain used to describe the difference between an Englishman and an American: A regular person is someone who does things because they *have* been done before. A teacher is someone who does things because they *haven't* been done before. We see students as what they are, but know that each of them must become what he or she can become.

Many of our students will come to us looking for goals, seeking a dream, but having no idea of what or how. In that case, we can dream for them. We as teachers thrive on that challenge as every day we live those words of George Bernard Shaw, made famous by former President John F. Kennedy: "You see things; and you say 'Why?' But I dream things that never were; and I say 'Why not?'" But we also know that dreaming for those students is only a start.

It is acting on those dreams with our hard work and dedication that can make them a reality. As Joel Barker held,

"Vision without action is merely a dream. Action without vision just passes the time. Vision with action can change the world." That's right, "change the world," or at least our little piece of it. And because of the limitless impact we have on our students now, and, through them, generations we will never know, we can truly change a bigger part of the world than we may ever realize. The boundaries of a teacher's inspiration and influence know no limits of time or place.

Inspire Them to Start to Dream for Themselves

Though a necessary start, our dreaming for our students is nothing more than a catalyst: the spark to light a fire. The fuel that will burn for their lifetimes, however, must come from them if it is to be true and long-lasting. But how do we start to encourage those first steps of dreaming? I believe we do it just as we would any other aspect of our teaching, whether it is for knowledge or an attitude: we take every opportunity to exude excitement and promise.

No better words exist to portray this than those of William Purkey when he wrote that the remarkable Leo Buscaglia "used the metaphor of knowledge being a marvelous feast. What the teacher can do is prepare food with great relish and care, sample it frequently, dance around the table at mealtime, and invite students to join the celebration!"

If we want our students to fulfill those words of Robert Louis Stevenson, "To be what we are, and to become what we are capable of becoming, is the only end of life," then we must get them to understand, as Carl Sandburg said,

"Nothing happens unless first a dream." What a valuable lesson that is for every child to learn. They must learn to cultivate dreams for who and what they wish to become. As Ariel Francos put so succinctly, "It's not what you are. It's what you want to be."

Is that a frightening thought for any young person? Is moving down that path a difficult choice? Is deciding to take those first steps of dreaming like walking through an open door into a dark, unknown room? Yes. But our students need to learn that "we cannot become what we need to be by remaining what we are." Sometimes that fear can be debilitating, causing many to feel it is safer to stay as they are than to risk dreaming of being more. I answer that with the words of Seneca: "It is not because things are difficult that we do not dare, it is because we do not dare that they are difficult."

Get Them to Dare Mighty Dreams

Once our students have started to think in terms of possibilities rather than probabilities, and taken those first steps of dreaming for themselves, we must urge them to start dreaming bigger dreams. After experiencing the freedom and exhilaration of dreaming, and the success that comes from steps (no matter how small) along the path to our dreams, they need to be coaxed into envisioning even mightier dreams. They must dare to think in terms they once thought unattainable, realizing that "only those who attempt the absurd achieve the impossible." Or as T. S. Eliot put it, "Only those who will risk going too far can possibly find out how far one can go."

Sometimes it's not envisioning *how far* we need to travel that becomes our mission but envisioning another path to get us there. That straight line we *think* is the best way to our mighty dream may be tried and true, but may not be the safest, best or most beautiful route. Often it is more about dreaming up a better mousetrap than how to get more mousetraps. Wonderful will be the moment when our students grow to understand and live by those remarkable words of Ralph Waldo Emerson, "Do not follow where the path may lead; go instead where there is no path and leave a trail."

Whether it's learning to dare to go further or dare to go a different way, the bottom line is for them to dream what they never imagined achievable so they can achieve what they only dreamed imaginable. As C. S. Lewis stated so exquisitely, "Aim at Heaven and you will get Earth thrown in. Aim at Earth and you get neither."

Once we get our students to dream big dreams, the largest challenge we face is to keep them focused on those dreams despite any setback, lack of momentum or temporary failure. They need to keep their eyes on the prize: the goal at the end of that dream. We must convince them that the small bumps along the road don't guide our path, they make it interesting. Like a racehorse wearing blinders so as not to get distracted by passing horses, our students need to ignore the distractions of disappointment, staying focused on the goal at the finish line.

If they turn back, quit or change course simply because the path gets difficult, or because others decide to go different ways, they will never discover their true potential. I think Omar Bradley said it best: "We need to

learn to set our course by the stars, not by the lights of
every passing ship." Those passing ships in life do offer
light, but the beacon of the stars must always be the
guide to that place where dreams help shape the destiny
of our students.

Final Thoughts

Why do we need to dream for our students and teach
them to dream? Simply because if we don't, quite possibly
no one ever will. Inspiring our students to dream gives them
the liberty to become ever more perfectly what essentially
they are. We can help them to *truly* understand the words
of former President Woodrow Wilson when he said, "We
grow great by dreams. All big men are dreamers. They see
things in the soft haze of a spring day or in the red fire of a
long winter's evening. Some of us let these great dreams die,
but others nourish and protect them; nurse them through
bad days till they bring them to the sunshine and light
which comes always to those who sincerely hope that their
dreams will come true." In that way they will learn to dare
to dream, and nourish and protect *their* dreams until they
see the sunshine of their tomorrows.

As with a diamond, each single facet of their dreaming
and "daring" may be modest in value, but the combination
of the facets becomes priceless — just like them! As Winston
Churchill stated so perfectly, "We make a living by what we
get, we make a life by what we give." What better to give
our students than the gift of dreams? What better indeed!

I would like to close with a poem that was given to me
some years ago by a student in one of my ensembles. In

its simplicity we can find the hopes of all those whom we
teach.

Shoot for the Moon

That time you asked me to shoot for the moon,
I knew it was important to you,
So I did,
But I failed.

That time you asked me to shoot for the moon,
You told me to try,
So I did,
And I failed.

That time you asked me to shoot for the moon,
I tried again because you made it sound so good,
And I did,
But I failed.

That time you asked me to shoot for the moon,
You lifted me half way there,
So I did,
And I failed.

That time you asked me to shoot for the moon,
Was only the first of many,
That I did,
But to fail.

That time you asked me to shoot for the moon,
Ended up being the start of a journey,
Though I failed,
But I did.

That time you asked me to shoot for the moon,
Showed me the way,
But to dream,
So I did.

And now that I've been there many times,
Though some I did fail,
That time you asked me to shoot for the moon,
Was the day I truly learned how.

EVERY PERSON HAS
A STORY

"Where are you off to this morning?" asked the young driver as we pulled away from the hotel en route to the airport. "New York City," I replied in a groggy voice, the result of a combination of jet lag and sleep deprivation. "How would you compare Oregon to New York?" he asked inquisitively. Fighting back a yawn, I responded by talking about how both places were wonderful. "I really want to visit New York someday," he stated, "but first I want to go to Japan." Now at 6 a.m., on three hours of sleep, it was hard for me to think, let alone talk, but I wanted to be friendly, so I replied with something like: "That's nice."

He continued with a brief life story: "Well, you see, I was born in California, then moved to Eugene for college, but I have spent a lot of time in Seattle. So because I have spent my life on the West Coast, I feel the need to explore other places. After I graduate, since I am studying Japanese, I want to teach for a year in Tokyo." He went on to speak of his studies, his dreams, his aspirations, his concerns, his fears and his hopes. As he talked, I listened more. As tired as I was, it just seemed so important. He was reaching out and I had to reach back. I forced myself to find the energy to communicate with this stranger whom I would probably never see again. He had a story, and I found myself actively listening to every word, egging him on for more. Fatigue lost out to connecting with a fellow human being.

By now I am sure you are thinking this story will turn to one where he tells me he was the victim of some terrible tragedy or he was suffering from an incurable disease. Nope. No talk of suicide or domestic violence. Nothing profound, devastating or bizarre. I'm certain that if the conversation had taken that turn I would have listened and communicated with all my heart. I would have counseled and commiserated with every fiber of my being. Isn't that what we teachers always do? But it didn't turn. This was just simple chatting about everyday life but I listened intently and thoughtfully. I wanted him to feel that I was interested. Truthfully, at first I was far more concerned with closing my eyes for twenty minutes on the way to the airport. But sharing time with that polite young man became important. Why? I don't know. I do know that I didn't want to let him down or make him think I was uninterested.

We arrived at the airport. He wished me a safe trip. I wished him well for his future. And as he walked away, he said, "I hope I see you again sometime." You know what, so did I. As I walked into the airport and wandered to my gate, a bad feeling came over me. I couldn't shake it but I also couldn't understand it. It was a combination of disappointment with myself, regret, opportunity lost, and introspection. In short, it was the feeling I get when I am *not* being the teacher I want to be or hope I can be. I was plagued by

it but didn't understand why that simple conversation with
a stranger would make me feel that way. It obviously hit a
nerve and got me thinking about it in relation to my teaching. What could that possibly have to do with my being a
better teacher?

Then, standing in line to board the airplane it hit me.
What troubled me was that I took the time and energy to
do that with a total stranger but hadn't taken the time and
energy to do that with every one of the students entrusted
to me. I knew in my heart that when students came to me
with a problem or crisis I attended to them. When a death
in the family, illness or divorce struck I would take the time
to talk. When a crisis of career choice or ability came to a
head I would try to reach out. When a relationship break-
up happened I would offer sympathy. That was not the
problem.

What bothered me so much was I knew that unless it
was a crisis, I was not always willing to make time just to
chat. About everything or nothing. I didn't know if my
principal flute player wanted to teach in Tokyo or if my
freshman clarinet student took Japanese. Truthfully, I didn't
know that about most of my students. But I knew that about
a young man whom I met for twenty minutes some 3,000
miles across the country. On a practical level, I understood
that part of the problem was time. I could certainly rational-
ize my concerns with a formula that went something like
this: time equals the number of students I have, divided
by the number of hours in a day, minus personal life crises,
multiplied by the square root of the ever-present feeling of
being away from my family too much, added to the inverse
of the sum total of time spent doing paperwork, answering

the phone, responding to email and attending meetings. Time just seems so elusive. Maybe time couldn't be found. But I knew I always found time when a student was rushed to the hospital, or for a student's brother's funeral, or to help a student who I feared would take his or her own life. Why was there not enough time just to chat? That conundrum seemed to be the quintessential example of *not* living life as if there were no tomorrows. I knew that formula was just a reasonable excuse and remembered a wonderful quote a friend gave to me, "Excuses are the nails to build a house of failure."

I hope, no, I pray my students know I care about them. Not just about their education but about their lives, about them as people. I know they mean so very much to me but do they know it? I think being there for them at times of distress is very important. Being there for guidance and counsel is as well. But the truth be known, I think the crisis of conscience I had at the airport reflects the fact that I think spending more time just chatting may be equally important.

I then realized this must be something I am very concerned about. Why else would it have disturbed me so? Enough negative, I thought. I was going to seize the opportunity. I needed to take positive steps, to move forward, to do and be better. I had to live those words of William Drayton, "Change starts when someone sees the next step." Thinking about how this all began I decided that the next day, a Monday morning, as I walked through the halls of the music building I would turn over a new leaf of chatting more. Instead of simply saying "hello" when I saw one of my students walk down the hallway, I would chat.

Well all I can tell you is that by about eleven o'clock that
Monday morning I overheard one of my students asking a
bunch of others, "Why is Dr. Boonshaft asking everybody
what language they're taking?" Hey, it was a start. Was it
easy? No, I guess I'm not a natural born chit-chatter. It was a
challenge. But as Joshua J. Marine asserted, "Challenges are
what make life interesting; overcoming them is what makes
life meaningful."

Over time I moved on to more lucid chitchat. I like to
think I am better at it now. Am I a model of what I would
hope to be? No! Am I better? Yes! Many of my students did
ask, "What's up?" I never told them. I thought it better just
to do it. But if I had answered, what I would have wanted to
say was, "Every person has a story. I just wanted to make sure
I found out what yours was." To put it simply, I have always
wanted to be a teacher who lived by the words of Frederick
L. Collins: "There are two types of people — those who
come into a room and say, 'Well, here I am!' and those who
come in and say, 'Ah, there you are.'"

When I get so busy I fall off the chatting wagon, I think
of that young man from Oregon. I wonder if he knows
he made me a better teacher on that early morning drive.
But even more important, do my students feel I became a
better teacher? I hope so. By the way, most of them took
Spanish. ■

"DOES YOUR BAND SOUND BETTER FROM THE BACK?"

I t was 1982. I was three hours into the first rehearsal of guest conducting this wonderful high school band in Oklahoma, and I needed a break. I walked to the back of the band room while the host director began rehearsing his band for the portion of the program he was to conduct. The back of the room was lined with large black wooden boxes that were used as packing crate-like cases when the band went on tour. They were arranged like giant *Lego* blocks to form a towering raked wall. I climbed atop those cases, leaned back and toweled off while resting. After a few moments of relaxing on this perch I had a realization. I had just spent the better part of the morning working with this band toward a good sense of ensemble balance. Though I didn't consistently hear that sound while conducting the group, I did hear it beautifully, vividly, now—in the back of the band.

I spent some time walking around the band as the students performed, listening *not* for whether the band was well balanced, but rather for how it sounded from each student's location within the band setup. I had always walked around my ensembles but I was always listening for whether I was getting what I wanted, not for how the *performers* heard it from their perspective. Though that may sound like semantic hair-splitting, it has truly made an enormous difference in how I attend to the teaching of ensemble balance.

It was at that very moment I became acutely aware of a problem. From where tuba players sit in the back of many ensembles, they almost always hear a *very* balanced, possibly ultra-balanced and blended sound. Think about it. Taking into consideration the omnidirectional or unidirectional nature of certain instruments, and seating designs that are often used, we ensure a wonderful sound from *that* vantage point: *the back of the band.* Think about it from that spot: the bass and tenor brass close by you with a sound that permeates the area like fog, trumpets in front of you "aiming" the sound away, French horn players directing that fantastically rich sound right at you, treble woodwinds a fair distance away with the highest voices farthest away. What do you have? The balanced sound we strive for. All too often, for many players, the well-balanced sound we describe and define is pretty close to what *they* hear when *we* say the band sounds *poorly* balanced.

Obviously, this is a gross oversimplification. And though I described this situation using a band as the example (mostly because I liked the quasi-alliteration of the title), it is the same with any ensemble. Of course depth of instrumentation, seating design, the quality of each performer's tone, characteristics of our rehearsal space, and our own preferences regarding tone and balance will play a large role in this issue, but it does point to a link all too often forgotten. We spend hours working on balance in rehearsals, we study methods and techniques to develop this skill, we invent warm-up exercises to practice a balanced sound, we impart to our players how important a balanced sound is to our success, we play recordings of fine bands, and we encourage our students to attend concerts and listen to recordings of professional ensembles.

However, even though we may compare and contrast "balanced" and "unbalanced" sounds in rehearsals, the missing link is that we often do not explain to our players that the sound we strive for is balanced from the front and that for much of the ensemble this will provide a very unbalanced, or sometimes hyper-balanced, sound to their ears. If left to their own natural, untrained instincts, ensembles will not produce a balanced sound, but is that totally due to lack of effort or understanding or because from where they sit it sounds pretty good?

Human nature being what it is, why should they work harder if it already sounds good to them? Depending on where they sit, an unbalanced (from the front) sound can sound just like those recordings of well-balanced ensembles we play for our students. Now I have always been an advocate of having recordings of remarkable bands playing as students walk in and out of rehearsal, but if the above phenomena is not explained that may compound the problem. Certainly we can attempt to fix some problems with changes in seating design, but all too often those changes make another problem worse.

Players must understand that what they need to develop and learn is what a balanced ensemble sounds like from *their*

seat. In other words, what it must sound like from their vantage point so they can contribute what is necessary for the
entire ensemble to sound well-balanced. It is not that we
need to strive for a different concept of balance or blend or
teach it differently, it is simply remembering that many of
our performers will be listening for a very different quantity
and quality of sound than that which we describe as our
goal. Once the balance we wish is achieved, we must have
our students lock that sound into their memories, as their
personal balance goals, even though it may sound unbalanced to them.

The story I referred to happened twenty-seven years
ago, and though it pointed out to me a very simple notion,
I think about it during almost every rehearsal. Though we
all have a different approach to — and ideal of — ensemble
sound, this simple idea may be helpful. The next time you
have a chance, walk to the rear of your ensemble and listen.
It is an easy quiz. Just ask yourself if your band sounds better from the back. ▨

WRESTLING A GORILLA

"Genius," wrote Thomas Edison, "is one percent inspiration and ninety-nine percent perspiration." Have you ever thought about that renowned quote? I mean truly *thought* about it, not just *heard* it? The "inspiration" part is straightforward enough, but what did he really mean by "perspiration"? Is it simply hard work? Probably so, but don't you think the effort he refers to must also include a healthy dose of perseverance? I can't help but believe Mr. Edison would have thought so. Perseverance, that resolve and determination to continue in the face of frustration, fatigue, resistance, obstacles, difficulty or failure, is quite certainly at the core of genius, but more important, it is at the very heart of teaching and learning.

Have you ever had one of those classes or rehearsals where nothing seemed to go right? You know, the ones which test your ability as much as your patience, where achievement seems distant and the chances of success in reaching your goal seem remote. On those occasions, students seem unmovable, ensembles seem unwilling to budge despite our best efforts. It's like trying to move a mountain or drag a mule. It's quite simply like a wrestling match of will, patience and stamina, stated best by Robert Strauss when he advised, "Perseverance is a little like wrestling a gorilla. You don't quit when you're tired, you quit when the gorilla is tired."

We all have those days, yet we all know tomorrow holds the promise of better. So we persevere, knowing the cause is too vital and the work too important to do anything less. We live the words of Publius who declared, "I can live with losing the good fight, but I can not live without fighting it." We practice the words of Margaret Thatcher who warned, "You may have to fight a battle more than once to win it." We heed the words of Cervantes who realized, "He who loses wealth loses much; he who loses a friend loses more; but he that loses courage loses all."

Whether it is the courage to persevere in the face of obstacles, the temporary failures of the moment, the difficulties of a situation, or the apprehension of an unplanned educational detour, it is the courage to persevere that can make all the difference in the lives of those whom we teach. It may mean having the courage to stay the course, adapt our approach, savor a tangent, remediate a concern, learn from a mistake or delight in an unexpected revelation. It may be any or all of those things; the only constant is courage.

Though remembering thoughts like those can help keep things in perspective, sometimes it's still a bumpy ride on the road of progress. Sometimes teaching feels like we are running at full speed straight into the wind. At those times the trick is to realize that in many ways our success in teaching is like an airplane on takeoff. That's right, an airplane on takeoff. Let me explain.

It would seem that our teaching would be best, most fruitful, when all is going as planned, students are with us and the proverbial wind is at our backs. Just like it would seem that the best chance for an airplane to lift from earth would be for it to have the wind at its back, helping to move it aloft. Not so. Not so at all. In fact, nothing could be further from the truth. You see, airplanes always take off *into* the wind. That's right: pilots steer their craft straight into as much headwind as they can. Why? Bernoulli.

More precisely, the Bernoulli Effect, which tells us that lift is created by the pressure differential above and below the airfoil shape of a wing. So the more air that runs across a wing — coming from that headwind — the better. Strange as it may seem, the more wind we get in our face, truly forcing our airplane into the path of most resistance, the easier we can soar to great heights. Maybe that's true in teaching as well?

Maybe those times when we need to wrestle gorillas can be more productive than we think, as long as we keep at it until the gorillas are tired. Maybe having the educational "wind" in our face can be stimulating and invigorating. Maybe our best teaching can be found on the path of *most* resistance. Maybe our teaching challenges are the "headwind" we need for our educational "lift." Maybe, just maybe, wrestling gorillas can be more wonderful, more joyous, more amazing than one could ever imagine.

Bel Kaufman, in her remarkable book, *Up the Down Staircase*, offers a poignant glimpse into the essence of perseverance. Threaded through the book are notes written back and forth between a new teacher and an experienced colleague about the frustrations of education. The new teacher, after many trying experiences, wrote "I am — more than a bit fed up. I once taught a lesson on 'A man's reach should exceed his grasp, or what's a heaven for?' I'm no longer sure that this is so; the higher I reach, the flatter I fall on my face. How do you manage to stand up?"

The response from her experienced friend, brought to her by a student, is as overpowering in its simplicity as it is in its truth: "Look at the cherub who is delivering this note. Look closely. Did you ever see a lovelier smile? A prouder bearing? She has just made the Honor Society. Last year she was ready to quit school. Walk through the halls. Listen at the classroom doors. In one — a lesson on the nature of Greek tragedy. In another — a drill on *who* and *whom*. In another — a hum of voices intoning French conjugations. In another — committee reports on slum clearance. In another — silence: a math quiz. Whatever...something very exciting is going on. In each of the classrooms, on each of the floors, all at the same time, education is going on. In some form or other...young people are exposed to education. That's how I manage to stand up. And that's why you're standing too."

Each time I read those glorious words, each time I am reminded of that remarkable quote by Browning referenced by the young teacher, I realize their truth and wisdom. We each must cherish our strength to persevere, to stand and face the wind, to reach beyond our grasp, to know the power of education and the promise of our mission. In that way for us as teachers our reach will always exceed our grasp, and that my friends is just what a heaven is for. So the next time those gorillas show up with thoughts of wrestling, embrace the possibilities and realize the importance. ▪

"WE'LL MAKE IT FUN"

There I was at a state music education conference, sitting outside a large exhibition hall. I was taking a break, relaxing quietly, when all of a sudden the all-state chorus comes walking by en masse. It turns out the students, all three hundred of them, were given this time to spend walking around the exhibits. Now I love doing that and I think it is a great idea, but I did hear several kids complaining the whole way in. The laments were strong and numerous.

That was until a group of young ladies walked by me. Instead of joining the chorus (sorry, I couldn't resist) of grumpy voices griping about this plan, one of them said, "It's okay, we'll make it fun."

I was shocked. No, I was flabbergasted. I don't know why, but in this day and age to hear a young person with sparkling optimism was so very wonderful. And for you pessimists reading this, she wasn't being sarcastic. She really meant it. I marveled as I watched and listened to this charming young woman convince her friends to make this event a positive one. She could have just as easily gone with the pack and complained her way through the time, but she didn't. She chose to make it fun.

Now the truth be known, she could have meant that they were going to burn the building down or trip old people for fun, but I doubt it. She didn't just say those words, she sold them. After they passed I sat there trying to figure out what made her that way. What made her say that and really mean it? I don't know, but I guess she was a product of her teachers and her parents. She must have learned it somewhere, and that somewhere was probably by seeing others say and do the same.

What a wonderful way to go through life: choosing to make boring or lackluster situations positive and worthwhile, yes even fun. Now before you start expecting smiley faces and rainbows on the next page assuming I have lost my charter membership in the Pessimists Club, I'm the first one to say that some things are never going to be fun no matter how you slice them. Getting a tooth drilled or having a flat tire is never going to be fun, never.

But how about practicing scales, rehearsing a tedious passage or learning a difficult skill? Do we make those things fun for our students? Do we show enjoyment when rehearsing frustrating spots? Certainly I know I can't always be happy or always make things fun but I wonder if I could do it more than I do. After stewing about that young lady's words I started thinking of all the rehearsing I've made my students do that I could have made more fun if I had only thought of her advice.

What a wonderful lesson for each of us: simply seizing every opportunity to make things not only hopeful and valuable, but fun, whenever we can, wherever we can, especially during those times that don't seem to be so. Now I hear her words every time I see boring and mundane around the corner, wondering how it can be made to be fun. I figure that if our students see us live those words, they too will learn that lesson, and what a wonderful gift that would be. ■

THE FOREST
FOR THE TREES

The football field runs north and south at our local high school, the home team bleachers standing high on the east side of the field, facing west. When I had all three of my children in the high school marching band, one of my favorite things to do each fall was to occasionally go to the school and watch an evening rehearsal. It just felt wonderful: the crisp air, the turning leaves, the sound of a drum cadence and the pride I felt watching my kids. I can't explain the joy but I guess some things just can't be explained.

However, being a band director to the core (no pun intended), I can't help but privately critique, analyze and evaluate everything I see and hear. I don't want to but I can't help it. I find myself focusing on every flaw. I listen for every wrong note and intonation problem. I watch for every misstep and gaffe. I myopically concentrate on the smallest of errors in an almost vicarious attempt to attend to every detail of the performance.

One such evening, I watched as the band was working diligently on its show. Being very early in the season, it was, quite frankly, pretty rough at times. There were lots of mistakes and lots of frustration. It seemed that even though I was fiercely concentrating, my telepathic efforts just weren't working. I was as frustrated as the kids and their teacher. With the patience of a saint, this wonderful educator would tell the kids to go back to a certain point in the routine and work through the set, always offering constructive criticism and praise. But let's face it, doing that over and over again, no matter how much praise is heaped on, can still have everyone seeing each error as if larger than life.

After the kids returned to their starting places facing the stands for another repetition, all of a sudden a very different command came out of the mouth of this teacher. With a firm yet joyful voice she said, "Everybody turn around and take a minute to appreciate the beautiful sunset." At that moment, as the students turned around, I looked up from the field to see one of the most magical, magnificent sunsets I have ever seen. The sky was ablaze with shades of red and yellow and orange that lit the evening sky with indescribable beauty.

There in front of my eyes I saw something even more beautiful than that sunset. I saw a teacher, a real teacher. For you see, I was so preoccupied with every flaw, concentrating on each wrong note, that I failed to see the wondrous sight before me. I was staring due west that entire time and never saw the forest for the trees. All I had to do was look up and notice. Sadder still, if I were their teacher that night, I don't think I would have told the students to do that, not because I wouldn't have wanted to, but because I probably wouldn't have noticed it.

On that fall evening, sitting in the stands of a football field, I learned a wonderful lesson from that amazing teacher. She heard every mistake and saw every foible, but would never — no *could* never — miss an opportunity to share beauty with those she was entrusted to teach. Wonder is all around us; I guess the trick is to always be looking for it, especially when it's right in front of us.

As I write these words I am on an airplane flying from San Jose to Las Vegas. I am also realizing just how hard it is to teach an old dog new tricks. For you see I have been so preoccupied with writing these words, tapping away on my computer, that I failed to take notice of the magnificent mountains that connect California with Nevada which have been in plain sight just outside my window for the past hour. Only at the end of my flight did I glance up and happen upon the sight. The snow-capped beauty, rugged simplicity, powerful majesty all mine for the taking if I had simply noticed sooner. It was a wonderful chance to gaze at remarkable splendor, sadly lost because I just didn't take the time to see it.

I wonder how many opportunities I have missed to notice astounding sights as I have passed through life. But even more worrisome, I wonder how many opportunities I have missed to point out beauty to my students. How many sunsets have I missed? How many mountains have I failed to share with my students? I hope to do better for myself and my students. I have vowed to remember the lesson I was taught sitting on those bleachers and work hard to live it. ▪

PERSONALITY

"It doesn't matter what brings a person, only what they leave with." So goes the wisdom of a wonderful Irish proverb. As teachers it really doesn't matter what brings students to us as much as the person they find when they get there. That person — that personality — who will capture their minds, spirits, imaginations and hearts: their teacher.

It has been said that teaching is 10% ability and 90% personality, and though that is surely an oversimplification, it does make the point we all know: the great teachers in our lives were somehow always able to connect with us, having personalities that were as powerful as they were sincere, as magnetic as they were concerned. Often that *power of personality* is what brought truth to the notion that the most important thing we as teachers make is a difference.

I often find myself thinking of those teachers in my life who made that difference, those beacons of inspiration, those models of the teacher I rarely am but the teacher I always hope to be. I dwell on their talents. I obsess over their methods. I detail their techniques but when all is said and done it always seems to be their personality that somehow made me want to learn. As Barbara Harrell Carson so eloquently stated, "Students learn what they care about, from people they care about and who, they know, care about them."

Certainly we can't underestimate all the other qualities that make for a remarkable teacher or diminish the importance of vast knowledge and profound talent, but we also can't underestimate the value of that indescribable characteristic known as *personality*. As Carl Jung so beautifully wrote, "An understanding heart is everything in a teacher, and cannot be esteemed highly enough. One looks back with appreciation to the brilliant teachers, but with gratitude to those who touched our human feeling. The curriculum is so much necessary raw material, but warmth is the vital element for the growing plant and for the soul of the child."

For some students it may be their teacher's passion for the subject matter, effervescence of spirit, enthusiasm for teaching or excitement about the joys of learning. For other students it may be their teacher's inviting manner, infectious humor, understated intensity or indomitable commitment. For others still, it will be facets of their teacher's personality no words can describe. The only commonality I have ever found — the only one that really matters — in all of those teachers in my life was their ability to lift up their students with the sheer strength of their personality as much as their talent, knowledge and ability.

For many young people it will be their teacher's profound guidance, embodying the words of Lao-Tzu who affirmed: "To lead the people, walk behind them." Or their teacher's modeling the wisdom found in the words of

Hermann Hesse when he asserted: "Happiness is a how, not a what; a talent, not an object." Or witnessing their teacher truly embrace the dignity of the phrase, "A different world cannot be built by indifferent people."

Maybe it's just that gift teachers have of being able to understand the student inside every person and the person inside every student. Maybe it's simply a teacher's capacity to care more than seems logical. Or maybe it's something only a teacher knows and a student senses. But whatever that mysterious thing we call personality *is*, however we try to describe it, one thing's for sure: it can make all the difference in the life of a child. A difference no words can describe short of paraphrasing the old adage: For those who understand, no explanation is necessary, for those who do not, none will suffice. ▪

ONE SIMPLE QUESTION

So there I was in front of a small auditorium full of teachers. After finishing a day of offering clinic sessions as part of a summer conference, I found myself the focus of an open forum to close the day's activities. You know, where participants can ask questions on any topic that interests them. I usually love those opportunities to share with my colleagues, finding that I learn far more from *their* questions than I can offer with *my* answers. Sometimes those questions can be straightforward and answered with simple facts. Sometimes they can be so open-ended as to allow only broad generalities. Sometimes they are thought-provoking probes seeking an opinion about questions I fear have no finite answer.

At that moment, however, I was asked a question that was nothing short of mind-boggling. I don't just mean it was a fact I didn't know or a topic I was clueless about. That happens all the time and I just plead ignorance. This was different. This one took my breath away with a physical reaction akin to panic. Why? Because this was a question for which I *had* to have an answer, an answer that governed all I do as a teacher. The question was at once as simple as it was profound, as complicated as it was powerful, as amazing as it was daunting. What was it, you ask? It was simply, "Dr. Boonshaft, what is the single most important thing we can do as teachers?"

After I caught my breath and stopped trembling at the magnitude of the query, my reaction was to ask if they would rather I tackle an easier question like the solution for global warming or the formula for peace on earth. Because, quite frankly, I think I may have had a better shot at answering those questions. Instead, I sat quietly thinking as hard as I could while looking out at the sea of eyes, those thoughtful souls waiting to hear my opinion. It *was* a great question; I only wish I had a great answer. But I didn't.

The minute I took to ponder the question seemed to last forever. It felt like an eternity as I reflected on possible answers. Was it to help students learn how to learn or to empower young people with tools for life and living? Was it to help children to reach their potentials or to light a fire of curiosity in all those whom we teach? Was it to help students find beauty in the world or to become well-rounded individuals? Was it to help society by planting seeds for future generations or cultivating human beings more in touch with their souls? Was it to help young people express themselves or learn the language of music and the skills needed to create it? At that moment my problem was that all of those answers and a myriad of others were correct. Yes, I thought, we need to do all of those things.

So I took a deep breath and rattled off a longwinded reply which included much of the above. As I finished my response, confident I had dodged that bullet, the gentleman who asked the question replied, "I asked for the *single* most important thing, not a list of things." Needless to say at that point I heard bullets whizzing by my head in every direction! So I thought a bit more as the audience sat patiently waiting for me to further make a fool of myself. At that instant, like a bad movie, memories of the great teachers in my life flooded my mind. I saw their faces, and more important, I felt their presence. Or better put, I felt how they always made me feel.

What was it about them? Was it how much they knew? No, I had many teachers who knew more. Was it simply that they cared about me? No, for I surely had other teachers who cared more. Was it how much they pushed me to achieve? No, others did that even more. Then it hit me. I had my answer.

I took another deep breath, this time with great satisfaction, smiled knowingly, looked out at my inquisitor and said, "I think the single most important thing we can do as teachers is *to make every single student feel he or she is incredibly important.*" How did I arrive at that seemingly simple answer? Well as I thought about all of those remarkable teachers in my life, yes, they knew a great deal, cared about me and pushed me to achieve, but there was something more, something far greater.

It was simply that in their presence I felt special, important and valued. They made me feel I really mattered and *that* feeling made me work harder, learn more, practice longer and fulfill that perception as best I could. How did they communicate that feeling? I have no idea, but I do know that with each word or action they sent the message loud and clear, reinforcing it over and over again. But as I reflect back on those teachers, the most amazing thing isn't

just that they were able to make *me* feel that way, it was that
they were able to make *every* student in their class feel that
way—every single one.

It reminded me of my mom; more specifically an event
shortly after her passing. My mother was a remarkable person. Her kindness and warmth radiated with a sincerity I
have rarely witnessed. She had a way of making everyone
she met feel special and valued in a way I can't describe.
I knew she had this ability, for surely I grew up nurtured
by it, but I never appreciated it more than the day of her
funeral. At the end of the service, in a receiving line, my
family greeted those who came to pay their respects to this
kind woman. One by one, Mom's friends offered their condolences as well as told their favorite story or recollection.

The most wonderful part, however, was that so many
people, after looking around to make certain no one could
hear them, whispered to us that they were my mom's *best*
friend. At the end of that day, as my sister and I reflected
back upon those conversations, we marveled at our mother's ability to make everyone—every single person—feel
extremely important. It was real, it was true, it was sincere.
She never needed to fake it or pretend because to her
people were special. She could find joyous qualities and
importance in just about anyone, and that couldn't help but
make people feel like they were her best friend. You know
what, truth be known, each of them probably was her best
friend. That's just how amazing she was.

That quality, that virtue, that special ability was shared
by all of the great teachers in my life who, each in their
own way, made me feel so very important. They went far
beyond just providing a sense of happiness or comfort; they

empowered me, encouraged me and emboldened me. They made me part of a prophecy they each saw that I couldn't help but work to prove true. It was a gift I cherished back then. It is a goal I have tried to make real in my teaching now. For surely students who are made to believe they are incredibly important can and will achieve just about anything.

I wish I could say I have succeeded in making every student feel that important; I have not. I haven't even come close, but I do try as hard as I can because I know how very important it is. Truly, what could be more important? Maybe people, like those great teachers, like my mom, are born that way, and I will never be able to meet that challenge. But I know what it meant to me and I hope to honor each of those remarkable influences in my life — and honor each of my students — by trying. A simple question indeed. ▰

MISTAKES?

Mistakes are bad. Right? Isn't that what we tell our students or at least imply to them and to ourselves? Playing a B-flat instead of a B-natural is a mistake. Coming in two measures early for a solo passage is a mistake. A bass drum strike in the middle of a movement marked "tacet" for the percussion is a mistake. True? Well, yes and no.

If correctness is the *only* measure our students or we learn to use then the answer is "yes." But if that is the case, little will be discovered, uncovered or explored. In other words, doing what we know works, *repeating* what's been done without error, may make the world *go around*, but *mistakes* make it go *forward*. What better lesson can we teach our students and how better can we show it than by example?

Don't get me wrong, I'm not saying that mistakes should be ignored or accepted. Not at all, but they should not be fatal to the learning process. Yes, there are times when wrong is wrong and that's it, but there are often times when wrong can be magnificent, wrong can be an opportunity for new possibilities, and wrong can expand our horizons.

As teachers, more important, as learners, we need to develop both abilities: the skill to replicate and the capacity to create. On the one hand we want our students to replicate *what is* with fewer and fewer errors. The goal then is to perform what they are working on as well as possible, reproduce success, copy excellence, imitate correctness, repeat for improvement and practice for consistency. Here mistakes are bad, problematic and unwanted.

On the other hand we want our students to create *what can be* with unconstrained enthusiasm and uninhibited abandon. The goal then is to create, originate, produce and envision what doesn't exist, whether it's devising improvements to what has already been done or conceiving innovative ideas about what has *never* been done. Here mistakes can be joyous fuel for a wildfire of creativity.

By way of example, name a few of the most famous towers in the world. I'll bet somewhere on your list was the Leaning Tower of Pisa. Why? Why is it so famous? Without a doubt, it is among the most famous buildings in the world not just *despite* but *because* of the mistake of its leaning to the side. By any builder's standard that is a mistake, but it is seen as beautiful and amazing to all those who behold it. I wonder if we would know of that tower in the town of Pisa if not for its odd sense of what's vertical. My guess is no. But the world has one more marvel in it because of that mistake.

Similarly, if I asked you to name some of the most successful inventions in office supplies in the past few decades, undoubtedly *Post-it Notes* would be high on the list. They have in many ways revolutionized office communication. They are everywhere, in every size, color and shape imaginable. Certainly whoever invented them didn't make a mistake. Or did he?

You see those sticky little yellow sheets of paper we all have on our desks began as a scientist's experiment. What was he trying to discover you ask? Surely it must have been the weakest glue imaginable, the most temporary of adhesives. Wrong; his goal was to invent the strongest glue possible. That's right, the ultimate permanent bonding agent. How's that for a whopper of a mistake?

Here's how it happened. Spencer Silver, a research scientist with the *3M Corporation*, was working on inventing a new, stronger, permanent glue. The result of one of his attempts was a glue that was just about the opposite of his goal. What he came up with was a glue that was not at all strong and not the least bit permanent. In fact he invented as weak and temporary a glue as one could imagine.

Some years later a gentleman by the name of Art Fry, another employee of 3M who knew of Silver's mistaken invention, had what turned out to be a pretty darned good idea while singing in his church choir. Each week, as the story goes, Mr. Fry used paper bookmarks to help keep his place in the hymnal, a strategy which worked well when they didn't *fall out of the book.* Then in a moment of what turned out to be sheer brilliance, Fry remembered the mistakenly invented glue he had heard about all those years earlier. The rest, as they say, is history.

So whether it's a tower in Italy, the little sticky notes on your desk or mistakes made every day in classrooms or rehearsals, they can lead to beauty, wonder, progress, courage, innovation and growth if we foster the mindset to allow that to happen. We can do just that by creating an environment that encourages students to attempt what they cannot do as well as to experiment with new ideas using what they can already do. In that way we empower students with the confidence to try without fear of failure as we encourage them to brainstorm and create without fear of ridicule. That freedom, that educational safety and security, can't help but bolster our students' willingness to expose themselves creatively, take imaginative risks and think productively.

With freedom to fail, or maybe better said, *with encouragement to fail*, students will have an entirely different attitude toward mistakes. Think about your own life. What would you have done differently if you had no fear of making mistakes? Would you have tried more experiments or accepted bolder challenges for yourself? Would you have worried less and envisioned more? Would you have savored creating what has never been as much as recreating what was? Would your creativity have been stifled less and excited more?

Now think about students who are asked to write a poem, improvise a jazz solo or draw a picture. They must decide to put themselves in a most vulnerable position. A positive environment can make them comfortable enough to attempt just about anything they conjure up, armed with a personal philosophy that failure is at the very least evidence of trying, and that simply trying is, in many ways, automatically succeeding. They are then as willing to learn something new as they are eager to experiment and create anew, living those words of General Douglas MacArthur: "Life is a lively process of becoming."

An unhealthy environment, however, may leave them gripped by fear. To those students, mistakes wait around every corner. They are so afraid of their mistakes of commission, ones which result from attempting something and "failing," that they often end up making more mistakes of omission, those made from simply not trying anything at all.

I guess it all comes down to the fact that educational safety can be a great teacher, as motivational as it is inspirational, whereas fear can be a terrible teacher, as debilitating as it is inhibiting. But with our help, our fostering a culture of confidence, our students can learn to conquer those fears and choose the path of taking educational risks over fearful stasis. Can that sometimes be a tough choice, especially for a young person? Does a willingness to try and create have its pitfalls? Would it be safer and easier to sit back and wait for others to blaze that creative path? Of course, but what students will soon learn is that taking those risks, educationally gambling on themselves, leading those creative expeditions is always better than following. Sure, you may smash into a tree or trip over a rock as you make your way along that trail, but you will be the first to see the vista at the top of the climb, unobstructed by anyone or anything. A view that is breathtaking for more reasons than meet the eye.

Quite simply, what I hope each of our students can embrace through their successes and their setbacks is embodied in a phrase, usually attributed to Søren Kierkegaard, my father taught me when I was very young. In fact it was the guiding philosophy in his life and through him has become so for me as well. Not a day goes by that I can't hear my dad's voice reminding me: "Life is a mystery to be lived, not a problem to be solved." It is a phrase I treasure. It is a phrase that affirms a healthy relationship with failures as much as it looks optimistically toward successes. A phrase as much about the perspective of what has been as it is the promise of what will be. A phrase that frames a life of optimistic wonder, creativity, curiosity and an attitude that enjoying the journey is as important as the destination.

We all know that balancing expectations of mastering material without errors on one hand, and creating and envisioning without boundaries on the other hand, can be a challenge. But let us never forget the rewards that balancing act can produce for us, for our students and for our world, for now and for the future, for this generation and for generations to come. Am I overstating the case? I don't know; let's ask the trumpet player, cellist or singer who someday creates a cure, solves an educational problem, composes a masterpiece, envisions the resolution to a legal dispute, designs a better town plan, conceives of a safer way to build bridges, establishes a remarkable charity, or resolves family disputes with inspired vision. All that and a whole lot more from simple mistakes.

By the way, isn't it strangely coincidental that the notes I wrote to myself for this chapter were jotted down on a bunch of *Post-it Notes?* Hmm ... ▨

GUARANTEED SUCCESS

Years ago, as he was leaving my office on his way to a final exam, a student said to me, "You'll have to excuse me, I have an appointment with success." I have always remembered those words and the confident smile that beamed from his face. Young people like that allow no limits to what they can learn or who they can become. Sadly I have also had those students who not just predict failure but determine it before they even start a task. For them, daring to dream is tempered by clouds of self-doubt, and risk is an uncomfortable gamble seldom taken. "And the trouble is," as Erica Jong so powerfully warned, "if you don't risk anything, you risk even more." Basically, it often seems that optimistic students think it's challenging to do the impossible while pessimistic students think it's impossible to do the challenging. But why?

Why do successful people believe they will succeed in most anything they undertake? What is the genesis of that kind of confidence, a confidence born out of far more than simple wishful thinking? Confidence for them is so deeply rooted in their being that failure is rarely even considered an option, let alone a probable outcome. Conversely, why do others seemingly assume failure from the start of any task, believing failure is not just a remote possibility but a foregone conclusion?

Why *do* some people see a goal as doable or achievable while others see the same goal as failure just waiting to happen? Are successful individuals simply born more confident and optimistic or is that a learned response? Over time, have they been conditioned by themselves and others to believe they can jump the hurdles of their goals and objectives simply because past attempts have proven they can? Essentially, has each successive achievement left them with no other conclusion than that accomplishing the goal at hand is assured?

Likewise, will numerous failed efforts condition some to assume the worst in all they attempt? Is that the learned response of those who have met with disappointment far too often? Is the enemy of their success simply being convinced of their failure? When that happens, do they basically set out to prove themselves correct: rationalizing a self-fulfilling prophecy they understand and can control?

As educators we can delight in the joy of teaching young people who believe themselves a success as they begin working toward any new objective, their enthusiasm for every new task sparked by their confidence. They are so sure of a positive outcome they welcome the work which lies ahead. But as wonderful as that is, little can be as heartbreaking as watching young people who are convinced of failure before they even make an attempt at a task.

What can we do? Can the firmly entrenched conditioning of a naysayer's past be changed? Can we as teachers alter the destiny of those who believe failure is their lot in life? Well I'm no psychologist, but surely I think we can help by embracing the remarkable words of Abraham Maslow who so profoundly stated, "What is necessary to change a person is to change his awareness of himself." Specifically, our students' *awareness of themselves* as either succeeding at what they set out to do or failing at all they attempt.

Though plain old "good teaching," reinforcing positive behaviors, individualized instruction, programmed learning and self-guided discovery go a long way toward nourishing the psyche of every child — and will serve the majority of our students well — for those few who have convinced themselves of their unquestionable failure, the remedy may be as simple as retraining them that success can be achieved by actually having them succeed, especially during those crucial initial steps toward a goal.

One of my favorite ways to do that goes beyond setting appropriate goals, individualizing objectives, ensuring accessibly small initial tasks or adding numerous steps along the way to make the progress seem easier. It doesn't just *include* students in setting objectives; it actually makes *them* arrive at the initial steps they will take toward that objective. No doubt for some students we will need to dictate those steps, ensuring their appropriateness, but other times having students make those early decisions can be the spark which helps move them along the path to self-confidence.

When that is the case, after clearly describing a new short-term goal to students and sharing its value, we can discuss and describe many different steps that will lead them toward accomplishing that end. Unquestionably, the *smaller* the *size* of the steps we suggest, the *larger* the *number* of possible steps we offer and the *greater* the *variety* of different approaches to accomplishing the task, the better.

Then, having armed students with a great number of possibilities, we ask them to write down the first two tasks they will undertake at the start of their educational journey. By having students individually determine the first two steps toward the goal, they are allowed to create objectives they know they can accomplish as they begin to take ownership of the work at hand, and ultimately their destiny.

By empowering students to choose the initial steps, those steps may be smaller than we wish, or easier than we wish, but they will usually be achievable. For it is the rare student who will choose a task he or she can't do. Yes, we will have to guard against those few overenthusiastic, overly ambitious or impatient children who will set impossible initial sights, setting themselves up for failure, but most students will be far more cautious than zealous.

The essence of this plan is that each student, with our guidance, will make those first steps small enough and easy enough as to be certain he or she can do them, thus ensuring success. It's as simple as that. After a while of doing this, students will start to feel the pride of accomplishing tasks and begin to feel they can succeed. Success will beget success. Accomplishment will beget accomplishment. If I am convinced I will fail, because I always have, what better start could there be toward reconditioning me than to have me succeed, and what better way to do that than have *me* decide the first two steps; steps I know I can accomplish?

Will this work for every child or for every goal? No, but when the situation is right it can plant seeds of confidence and positive self-determination for those in need of proving to *themselves* they can succeed. Will there be setbacks? Of course. But as Ralph Waldo Emerson reminds us, "Our greatest glory is not in never failing, but in rising up every time we fail." I guess for those pessimistic learners the trick is getting them to envision success as an option, let alone a probable outcome.

For many young people, like most of us, it's often not the goal we set that gets the better of us but the steps we take to reach that goal, especially those crucial initial steps. Remember, "Nobody trips over mountains. It is the small pebble that causes you to stumble. Pass all the pebbles in your path and you will find you will have crossed the mountain." Whether we choose the steps taken toward an objective, or our students help choose them, if those tasks are easy enough that students know they can "step over" those pebbles of learning, before they know it those mountains of education will be behind them and they will be convinced of the words of Virgil who simply observed, "We can because we think we can."

Kurt Vonnegut, Jr. stated, "We are what we imagine ourselves to be." We can apply that remarkable sentiment to our teaching as either a warning about students who doom themselves to failure because that is what they imagine themselves to be, or as a harbinger of success for those students who can imagine themselves in no other way. We just have to get each student to understand, paraphrasing the words of George Eliot, that it's *never too late* to become the person you could have been. ▪

The Right Tool for the Job

Though educational trends, jargon, methods, buzzwords, approaches, techniques, materials and technology seem to continually change, some fundamental truths remain fixtures in teaching and—more important—in learning. Yes, we have developed new technologies to encourage students to practice, new materials for reinforcing concepts, new philosophies of how to assess learning, new ways to accommodate different learning styles, new designs for merging diverse educational content, and the like.

But when it comes to the business of getting a child to be able to physically do something new, the initial learning of how to do a new activity or technique, I always come back to a brief moment I had in a class many decades ago while in undergraduate school. "Just remember," my professor said, "no matter how complicated we try to make it, it all boils down to the fact that we really have only three ways to *teach* a child *how* to do something: trial and error, verbal or written instructions, and imitation." The older I get the truer those words seem to me. It may be too simplistic, but so is the wheel, and that's worked out pretty well. The trick, it seems to me, is using the most appropriate of those for any given situation, using as many of them as possible and understanding the benefits and shortcomings of each. After all, the wheel is a magnificent device but probably not the best choice as a tool for getting to the moon.

Verbal and written instructions allow us to codify — step by step — how a student will learn a new action, making certain all necessary steps are included and are in the best sequence. Written instructions also allow our directions to be followed even when students are working on their own. Instructions are logical, orderly, neat, precise and easy to use and monitor. Instructions are ideal in many situations and for those reasons listed above we often gravitate toward using them, but they aren't without their problems.

Let's take an easy example. Using verbal or written instructions, teach a group of children how to make their first peanut butter and jelly sandwich. How complicated could that be? Let's pretend you started by giving each of them a box containing everything they'd need. Go ahead, after all it's only a peanut butter and jelly sandwich.

If you're like me, you came up with something like, "Place the box on a table, tape-side up. Open the box. Take everything out of the box. Spread two spoonfuls of peanut butter onto a slice of bread. Then spread two spoonfuls of jelly onto a second slice of bread. Put both slices together. Eat."

Pretty simple, right? Well if we assume the children we are instructing have had past experience with those ingredients, other sandwiches and culinary tasks, so they can transfer that previous training to this application, yes. Or if we have prepared this learning with many lessons defining and describing the ingredients and actions, yes. But if not, our instructions may pose more questions than answers and yield more blunders than successes. Why? Because in this case, as in any teaching, our success often rests with our ability to put ourselves in the shoes of our students, assuming they know nothing, and to prepare, label and explain each and every step along the way so it can be used for future learning.

So now let's try those directions again, assuming nothing: "Good morning, class. Today you are going to make your first peanut butter and jelly sandwich. Everything you need is in front of you in what is called a 'box.' Make sure the box is on your desk with the shiny clear stuff that sealed the box, called 'tape,' pointing up. Peel off that tape. Open the box completely by bending back the 'flaps,' or folds which closed the box. That will expose all of the items packed into the box. Next, take each of those items out of the box and place them on the desk, starting with the bag full of 'slices'—or cut pieces—of soft, white squares called 'bread,' then the glass jar of purple-colored stuff called 'jelly,' the jar of brown-colored 'peanut butter,' the flat round thing which is a 'plate,' the bright silver-colored metal tool that is sharp on one side and has a point at the end called a 'knife,' and finally the other silver-colored metal tool with no point we call a 'spoon.'

"Let's start with the plastic bag of bread. Start by holding the end of the bag that looks like a tail with one hand, while with the other hand you turn the twisted piece of metal in the direction which loosens it. Remember that if the piece of metal, called a 'twist tie' gets tighter you must turn it in the opposite direction. Once the twist tie comes off, reach into the bag and remove two slices of bread. After that is done, we must close the bag of bread by holding the end that looked like the tail in one hand as you turn the bottom of the bag around and around with the other hand. That will close the bag and create a small area of tightly crimped plastic bag for you to place the twist tie back onto by twisting it until tight.

"Pick up the jar of peanut butter, so that the top or 'lid' is pointing up. Holding the side of the jar of peanut butter near the bottom with one hand, grab the lid with the other hand. You can then open the jar by turning the lid so your hand spins counterclockwise, or in other words the opposite way the hands of a clock turn, while holding the bottom of the jar still. If the lid doesn't loosen, try turning the lid in the other direction."

Need I go on? Frustrating, isn't it, and at this point, after all that, we only have an open jar of peanut butter and two slices of bread laying somewhere. Didn't you find yourself getting more and more annoyed as you fought off the desire to say, "Forget it, just starve!"

You probably also found yourself thinking this is not realistic, for who would attempt teaching something like this without some preliminary training or preparatory foundation, and the ability to make some assumptions about previous knowledge or skill. Truth is, if you reread those directions, I made many such assumptions, such as an understanding of: desk, sandwich, shiny, clear, seal, up, completely, pointing, peel, open, bend, close, expose, back, items, packed, start, bag, all, full, pieces, cut, jar, the color purple, the color brown, flat, round, square, soft, bright, the color silver, the substance metal, tool, sharp, side, point, end, grab, plastic, full, hold, glass, tail, hand, other, turn, twist, loosen, tighten, opposite, off, into, remove, one, two, close, hold, direction, clock, bottom, around, small, area, tight, crimp, pick up, top, near and spin, let alone that they are breathing. It's amazing how often we make assumptions without even knowing it.

For us as teachers it's remembering that though *we* can do the task at hand with-our-eyes-closed-in-the-dark-hands-tied-together-while-solving-a-crossword-puzzle, because we have done it so many times, for our students each facet of any task must be detailed and defined. The success of our verbal or written instructions depends upon our ability to itemize every step of the new action, adequately describe those steps and then correctly sequence those steps in the most efficient way. All the while we must remember the importance and expediency of labeling what students learn so it can be used again without explanation, readying them for learning with adequate preparatory material, and helping them to use their previous training by transferring what they already know or can do to new situations.

Though verbal or written instructions, those step-by-step directions, are usually the first tool we metaphorically grab when teaching—because they are so perfect for learning many tasks—they are often not the best tool for the job, as is obvious with our peanut butter and jelly sandwich example.

As to trial and error, though it is the perfect tool for learning such skills as improvisation and composition where creativity is as important as correctness, for tasks like our sandwich, can't you just picture trial and error yielding more jelly on the ceiling than on the sandwich, and hands covered in "peanutty" goodness?

So for tasks such as our sandwich it's pretty clear how much easier it would be to use imitation. Think about teaching students the concept of characteristic tone on their instruments. What could be better than imitation? Just try describing the tone of an oboe with words; it doesn't work real well. Simple modeling so often is the easiest, but more important, the more effective and faster tool.

Obviously, more often than not we will use all three techniques successively or simultaneously in our teaching, such as *demonstrating* how to put together a trombone as we label the parts and sequence the step-by-step *instructions*. Or we may teach students the *directions* and rules for writing a harmonic progression then have them use *trial and error* to explore and master the undertaking.

Though rarely will only one of those three teaching approaches be used alone, examples such as our sandwich point out the importance of preparing material, not making incorrect assumptions, labeling, transfer of training, modeling and self discovery in education. So the next time we reach for those instructions, assuming they are the best tool for the job, we might want to remember how difficult, frustrating and time-consuming it was to give instructions for something as simple as a peanut butter and jelly sandwich to someone who doesn't know what one is.

THE BAR

I'm guessing *that* title got your attention! No it's not the "corner" one, it's the one we set for our students. That bar of expectations we constantly raise higher and higher. Without a doubt, of all the balancing acts a teacher must perform, that one has to be one of the most difficult. But of all the responsibilities we have, few could be more important.

We all take our students as we find them, assessing their abilities and potential, and chart a course for their growth. Being certain we factor in physical, mental and emotional readiness as well as appropriateness of material and concepts, we map the journey that will be their educational future. Armed with where they are and where they're going, we set our expectations: expectations for behavior and deportment, expectations for practice and preparedness, expectations for effort and enthusiasm.

Those expectations, to me, are fairly straightforward and easy to assert. However, setting expectations of *achievement* — those standards of what we find an acceptable level of performance and what is not — are where the real challenges lie. Expect too much, we run the risk of frustrating them, burning them out, squelching their enthusiasm or causing them to doubt whether they can ever succeed. Expect too little and they will progress too slowly, if at all.

So if we set that bar too high or continue to raise it too fast they may just give up from exhaustion or disappointment as we try to move them further or faster than appropriate. But if we set it too low or raise it too slowly they may give up from boredom or monotony as we offer little challenge or opportunity for growth.

The hardest of balancing acts, indeed. The tiniest line separates success and failure, ours and our students'. Surely we have all had teachers who relentlessly pushed us way too fast or demanded far too much. Sometimes we rose to the occasion but sometimes we ended up hating the entire endeavor. Equally sad, however, is the teacher who can't move us along fast enough or far enough to keep us interested and eager. Often in that case we lose interest, no matter how able or adept we are.

But when I search my past, the teachers I loved the most always seemed to know how much to push me and how far was far enough. They never let "grass grow under my feet" with complacency, never let me grow disillusioned with frustration, rather they balanced those two while always helping me savor my successes and enjoy the journey. Each of *us* does that for *our* students every single day.

Though I know the value of staying the course and trying my best to walk that fine line, I must admit there are times I question whether I have gone too far, asked for too much, especially in large ensemble rehearsals. I wonder if I have pushed my students beyond what is reasonable, asking their performance to reach further than that which they can confidently count on. I don't have reservations about pushing them as far as possible; I do worry, however, about the consequences. Have I helped my students surpass their assumptions of what is possible by allowing them to work beyond what *was* thought to be their ability, now able to do what they once thought was impossible? Or have I set them up for disappointment by asking them to perform at a level they can't consistently maintain with comfort?

It's not that I worry about whether I have pushed them so far they may fall off a *firm* cliff; rather, it's that I have pushed them to a place where the cliff is made of crumbling rocks that are as insecure as the day is long. Have I set the bar so high that missing it is a real possibility? It is living with the aftermath of that I fear.

I remember one such occasion in particular. A wonderful weekend honors band festival was drawing to an end. In fact I was walking from my hotel to the convention center concert hall on what was a beautiful spring day. There I was delighting in the weather while fond memories of our rehearsals flooded my mind. Then that joy began to turn to worry as I thought of specific moments in the program I feared could turn south on us. Would the students be able to do what they wanted to accomplish? Could they jump over the bar I helped set? Or did I put them in harm's way, allowing them to try to do what we all knew was little better than the musical equivalent of flipping a coin?

As I walked farther, worry turned to fear, fear turned to panic. *I* didn't care if a few booboos made their way into the performance, for I knew what *really* mattered that weekend had already happened in rehearsals. My concern was for specific students who had exposed solos or subtle crucial moments that were "dicey." I saw their faces, especially two or three of them in my mind and feared I had put them out on that rickety precipice.

As I got closer to the hall the lack of confidence I had in my walking that fine line of expectations grew worse. By the time I got there and opened the door to the lobby, I was really shaken. As I entered the building I was met by a large group of students jubilantly waiting to take the stage. As I talked with them I noticed one of the kids I worried the most about standing quietly in the crowd. I smiled at her, she faintly smiled back. Now my panic turned to dread. What had I done?

So I motioned to her to come over so we could move off to the side to talk in relative privacy. I asked if she was excited about the concert. She smiled and said she was. I then went on to tell her (lying through my teeth) how confident I was in her playing this one very exposed and difficult passage. She offered a halfhearted grin, and said, "I hope I can do it." After telling her how much I believed in her, I went on to say that her performing it beautifully in rehearsals mattered most and that I heard her do it, every member of the ensemble heard her do it, and most important, she heard herself do it. My speech was met with little more than another grin.

I then looked her in the eye and asked, "Did I push you too far? Did I raise the bar too high, higher than you can comfortably jump?" To that she replied, "Never. I look at it this way: you raised it so high that even if I can't jump over it, I can walk under it standing pretty tall, and that's good enough for me."

So within reason, we should keep working to raise the bar higher and higher, knowing that if we get the bar high enough it doesn't matter if they occasionally can't jump over it; they don't have to as long as we make sure they know they can walk under it standing proud and tall.

I can still remember that moment as if it were yesterday. I was rendered speechless by her wisdom. I was humbled by her character. I was astounded by her grace. Hearing her words I knew it really didn't matter what happened during that concert; she had already learned all that was truly important, and taught me far more.

ANOTHER WAY

The good teacher teaches information, the excellent teacher teaches what students need to know, the great teacher teaches students why they need to know it, but the extraordinary teacher makes students want to learn it. Though we need to do all of those things, I think the last one—getting kids to want to learn—can pose our greatest challenge. We can illuminate, inspire and reward. We can praise, push and explain. But sometimes it still proves difficult, difficult indeed. At those times it can be tempting to flirt with giving up, deciding that simply teaching the material is good enough. Often though it comes down to our simply finding another way, a way that makes students want to learn even if they don't realize why. Let me share three stories that may help describe what I mean.

For many years the salmon canning industry struggled with meager sales especially when compared to those of canned tuna fish. They tried, seemingly in vain, to garner some of the remarkable success and market share of that popular staple of the kitchen. However, it seemed that people were so used to the mild whitish look of the canned tuna that when they opened a can of salmon and saw pink they were turned off. Every attempt to get people to buy canned salmon suffered from the fact that it was pink. Many consumers even thought the product must have started white, like tuna, turning pink while in the can, almost as if going bad. Many companies gave up on even trying to market it.

But then someone decided there had to be another way: there had to be a way to get the average person to want to buy canned salmon. The result was one company launching a marketing campaign with a new slogan on every can of their salmon. It was a campaign that almost single-handedly changed the industry and bolstered sales to new heights of success. What, you must be wondering, could have done that? What could have gotten people to completely change whether they would buy the pink product? What words could have changed the mindset of so many people? Ready? The new label read: "Premium Canned Salmon: *Guaranteed to Stay Pink In The Can.*"

Amazing isn't it? Those simple words got people to buy canned salmon. In one fell swoop many people went from uninterested in the can of pink fish to seeking out that brand because it *guaranteed* them it would stay pink in the can. Instantly the product went from reviled or ignored to prized and sought after, all because someone found another way to the goal of *getting people to do something*.

The next story begins at a museum. Though there were signs all around the building nicely asking people to "Refrain From Touching" the works of art, people just couldn't resist laying their grubby little hands on every piece of treasured sculpture or antique furniture. So the curators decided to put signs directly next to each piece of art stating clearly: "Do Not Touch." That too failed. Next they placed attendants around the facility to ask patrons not to touch the objects. As audacious as it sounds people still seemed to go out of their way to grope the art.

At the point where most people would have given up in defeat, succumbing to the fact that this could not be stopped, someone found another way. No more guards, no more hassling offenders, no more threatening customers. In fact the next day every sign around the building asking people to "Refrain From Touching" was removed. So too the "Do Not Touch" signs next to each object of art. What replaced them? What new threat could stop this behavior? What could get people to stop their previous actions? New signs were hung that simply read: "Warning: Toxic Chemical Preservatives Have Been Sprayed On All Objects. Seek Immediate Medical Attention If You Accidentally Touch Anything." Talk about finding another way! Instantly, a new solution solved an old problem: *getting people not to do something*.

The last story takes place in a middle school where some of the young women who attended the school, seemingly excited about their newfound use of makeup, thought a clever prank would be to "kiss" the bathroom mirrors after applying vast quantities of lipstick, leaving lipstick splotches all over each mirror. After every incident the administration threatened punishment and tried to scare the culprits with lengthy missives and lectures, all to no avail. It seemed that with each threat the problem grew and spread. It also seemed nothing could solve the problem, leaving the staff little choice but to remove the mirrors.

That was, until one day when the principal *found another way*, calling for a large group of young ladies most suspected of the offense to a meeting in one of the bathrooms adorned with lip prints. Also in attendance was the head custodian. "Ladies," the principal began, "this immature, foolish, ridiculous nonsense of kissing the mirrors has to stop." As you can imagine, those words were accompanied by much eye-rolling and smirking from those assembled. "In addition," she continued, "it takes so much time and effort for our custodians to clean each mirror. In fact, I'd like you to see just how hard it is for them to clean those mirrors every day." At that signal from the principal, the custodian took the dirtiest mop he could find and swished it around in the filthiest toilet for a few moments before slapping it up on the mirror with vigorous scrubbing motions. Almost as fast as all of the girls gasped, covered their mouths in pseudo-nausea and felt sick, the problem was solved.

So sometimes it's simply that we must find another way to get our students *to do* something we *want* them to do, or *not to do* something we *don't want* them to do. Either way the solution may rest with how creative we can be as teachers.

As Albert Einstein reminds us, "The significant problems we face cannot be solved at the same level of thinking we were at when we created them." Possibly, the significant solutions we seek for our students cannot be found when they are at the same level of thinking as they have been. The answer may lie in simply finding another way. Think about sushi for a moment. I figure it this way: if some creative marketing person could not only discover a way to get people to try eating raw fish, but want to do it and pay a premium for it, I can figure out a better way to teach my students to do — or not do — just about anything.

Finding a way to get a principal to understand that rehearsals are hard work and focused educational time becomes an invitation to have the principal narrate a piece with the orchestra, thus seeing firsthand the process as well as the product.

Finding a way to get beginners to practice more gives rise to the teacher *limiting* the amount of time they are *allowed* to practice, increasing that amount of time gradually with great fanfare and celebration as the students earn the privilege to practice more. Now this does require acting worthy of an Oscar, but remember, someone once figured out a way to convince many people to pay for the privilege of going to a gym to sweat!

Finding a way to get parents to realize that students need to be on time and prepared for rehearsals turns into a special rehearsal where parents are invited to sit next to their child (maybe in a gym or other large space), offering them a chance to see and hear the work at hand and the rigor necessary for success.

Finding a way to get sixth-graders to practice a sheet of exercises or a certain piece may be to let it slip that the eighth-graders are currently playing it.

Who knows, maybe telling students they may not be ready to practice something may get them to practice it. Warning people they may not be able to do something may be the way to get them to work at doing it. Allowing a class to "overhear" you tell a colleague about a future pop quiz may just get students to learn certain material better than announcing it. Giving someone the freedom to do something may be the fastest way to get them to stop doing it.

Will these attempts always work? Surely not. Does thinking a different way require extra effort? Of course. Will we always be able to outsmart, use reverse psychology or manipulate the situation the way we want? No. So why try? Because what we do and those we are entrusted to teach are *that* important. Would it be easier to continue our usual course? Yes, but the next time you are in the market and pass the aisle with the canned salmon, or go to a museum, remember that sometimes finding another way can be the best way. ▪

A BOWL OF WHAT?

L et's try an experiment. A little test, if you will. Quickly read through the following directions: start by driving down Route 26, after the third traffic light turn left, pass two houses and make a left at the stop sign. Drive until you see the pink elephant reading a newspaper, turning right at the next traffic light. After driving nine miles, turn right on Route 94, then left onto Route 91, then another right onto Route 93. After you pass the sixth driveway, make a left on Route 19.

Now close your eyes and think back to the paragraph. What do you remember? I'll bet you don't remember many of the route numbers or which way you were to have turned when you got to them. I bet you don't remember how many driveways you were to have passed or how many miles you were to have traveled before turning. But I bet you do remember one thing. That's right, the *pink elephant reading a newspaper*.

Let's try another one. Read this list as fast as you can: a basket of tomatoes, a bushel of carrots, a plate of beets, a box of cucumbers, a bag of strawberries, a bowl of dancing pickles, a container of oranges and a case of apples.

Recite the list. Which did you remember and which did you forget? If I had to guess, you remembered the bowl of dancing pickles and forgot much of the rest. But far more important, which one do you think most of our students would remember? Why did we remember the pink elephant or dancing pickles? Well probably because they were absurd, unusual, humorous or bizarre. I guess it's human nature for us to remember that which is different, makes us laugh or is unexpected. Though I guess on some level I've always known that, as a teacher its power became abundantly obvious to me on one specific day.

One spring semester I was teaching a music education class at the university. It was a very demanding course which required the students to learn an immense amount of material. After a couple of months it came time for the midterm exam. I warned the students to know all of the material we covered in class as well as the assigned readings from two books. So each of them set out to study and remember vast quantities of information as well as how to use it. Two weeks later the students took the exam.

That evening I started to grade the twelve-page test taken by each of my thirty students. I started working my way through each of their answers, saddened by errors I had to correct, elated by responses that were precise. I had only gotten to page six of the first exam when I was hit with a most bizarre and disconcerting answer. In response to a question asking students for their opinion about a certain approach to solving a problem, one student responded, much to my horror, "it stinks." (In truth it was a bit nastier word which I'd rather not repeat here.) I couldn't believe it. I was left wondering why this young man would have given an answer that was so brusque and unprofessional. Why indeed.

After finishing his exam I moved on to the next one. As my eyes read that same question I gulped in disbelief as I read the same answer. Test after test, student after student, I read the same awful answer. Then it hit me. I realized why all of my students gave that answer. It was because I said it. That's right, *I* said it. In remembering back to the class when we discussed the topic, I could hear myself offering my opinion with those exact words for emphasis. I couldn't believe it: of all the answers they chose to remember, of all the times they had flawless recall of my precise statement, it had to be those words. But they did; every one of them.

Why? I guess the impact of hearing a college professor use those words was indeed memorable. My slip of the tongue strangely helped students remember the topic and use those less-than-perfect words as the launching point for their opinions. Do I wish I had found better words to express my thoughts? Yes. But then I am left to wonder if my students would have remembered the topic as well.

The answer to yet another question on this exam had me giggling in amazement. I had asked my students to describe how an egg carton could be used as a teaching tool, reflecting back to a discussion we had in class about a neat way of developing kinesthetic memory for a specific technique by holding an upside-down egg carton. Remembering the odd picture of me holding an egg carton in class was enough for them to remember the idea. That made sense, but what got me was the extra bit of information they all added to the end of their answers: "Remember to tell students to bring in an *empty* egg-carton."

Why did they add that bit of information? Because I told them a story about a teacher friend of mine who used this approach but regretted the day she forgot to tell her students the egg cartons they were to bring to school had to be empty. For my students, remembering me tell of the horror and disbelief of this teacher as she watched an entire dozen eggs dump onto the floor became unforgettable. The smashed yolks, broken shells and sticky mess were too vivid to forget.

Reflecting upon that exam and those specific answers made me stop and think. What can we do to make important information more memorable for our students? How can we present material so it is unforgettable? Surely every fact we teach can't be accompanied by a humorous anecdote, but what can we do to help our students remember that which is important? Whether it's using a funny mnemonic device, a catchy slogan, a joke, a story or some out-of-the-norm way of presenting the material, we can help make learning more enjoyable and, more important, memorable.

It's funny how with only a bit of thought I can remember odd things that have helped students remember. There was that day in a band rehearsal I told a percussionist that the way he was playing his part sounded like "bad disco," later to see that he had drawn a picture of a disco ball with an "X" through it to remind himself of the error. Or the day I realized that most every student in the band had written the word "something" at a spot in one piece. Why? Because once while rehearsing that spot in the work, in frustration I said, "Don't just sit there, write *something*." That they did. But the amazing thing was from that day forward they never forgot what I actually wanted at that moment in the piece. They might have thought they were being cute but they were actually making it memorable.

Maybe whether our students remember or not is more in our hands than we may think. Maybe the trick is to make what we want them to learn *unforgettable*, rather than simply ask them to *remember* it. Maybe a healthy dose of pink elephants reading newspapers or bowls of dancing pickles can be more powerful for our students than hours of memorizing. Just remember, the egg cartons are to be empty when students bring them to school! ▩

"It's Nice to
Be Nice to the Nice"

It was another one of those days that started at 4:45 in the morning, still pitch black outside when the taxi pulled up to my house to take me to the airport. Now traveling as often as I do, going to the airport at that hour doesn't usually bother me very much but on that particular morning I wasn't in much of a mood. Well truthfully I *was* in a mood, it just happened to be a bad one. You see, strange as it may sound, the night before I had arrived home at around midnight *from* the airport after another trip. That's right, figure in unpacking, repacking, breakfast and a shower and I had a grand total of about two and a half hours of sleep. Not that my lack of shuteye was a good excuse for being grumpy but it surely was the cause.

So I jump in the taxi and head off to the airport, sadly with my bad mood in tow. Though I hate to admit it my surly attitude got the better of me. I heard myself being short with the driver but I just couldn't muster anything better than far-less-than-friendly. I wasn't trying to be mean but I just couldn't seem to make myself get any nicer.

Then it happened. After several minutes of my kindly driver asking questions and making polite small talk and my responding in a manner best described as cranky, he said, "I can't tell you how wonderful it is to have such a nice customer this morning." As his words registered in my mind I almost looked around the cab wondering where that *other* customer he was talking about was sitting, for he surely could not have meant me. But, he did mean me. Almost instantly my attitude changed. A smile came to my face as I thanked him. Kindness came to my voice as I said I was sure everyone was nice to him. It was as though he had flicked the switch in my mind to turn on a good mood.

I know this sounds simplistic, silly and like a scene from a mediocre feel-good movie, but it's true. My bad attitude vanished as *I made his statement true.* My surly disposition changed as I began living up to his compliment, making what might have started as a bit of a fib on his part become reality. I could not help but prove him right, not because I had to, but because I wanted to.

For the rest of the ride this kindhearted older gentleman regaled me with some pretty amazing stories of how nice some customers had been and some equally amazing stories of how cantankerous others had been. Then at one point in a story he paused, looking thoughtful and said, "You know, it doesn't cost anything to be nice, right?" I chimed in with polite agreement, but the truth be known, his words rang in my head for the rest of the day. I could not stop mulling them over and over until I realized that not only was being nice free, it was contagious, disarming and uplifting.

As grumpy as I was, that sincerely kind cab driver's statement about me being nice made my lousy mood disappear, lifted my spirits, brightened my disposition and gently gave me little choice but to fulfill that prophecy. In short, his kind attitude was contagious and I caught it.

At that moment I was reminded of an episode of the television series *M*A*S*H* in which the commander of the mobile surgical hospital, Lt. Col. Henry Blake, had become smitten with Miss Nancy Sue Parker, a young lady half his age who came to visit the camp. The evening of her first day on the base ended with a trip to the Officer's Club for a nightcap. The scene began with two of the hospital's senior officers, Major Margaret Houlihan and Major Frank Burns — both of whom strongly disapproved of their commander's behavior — sitting at a table in the club as the colonel and his guest arrived. Realizing they would have to greet the young women, the two majors agreed they needed only to be polite, nothing more, or risk looking as though they condoned the colonel's behavior.

As Col. Blake introduced the perky, adorably sweet young woman to the pair of majors, the young guest gleefully spoke of how nice everyone at the camp had been to her. At that moment, a bit smitten himself, a starry-eyed Major Burns — dead set on being as curt as possible — helplessly blurted out: "It's nice to be nice to the nice" in the cheeriest voice imaginable.

Doesn't that have to be one of the dumbest sentences ever spoken? But as silly as it sounds, as cutesy as it may be, it's also true. It really is nice to be nice to the nice. In fact I think it may be *more work* to be mean to someone who is being nice, *harder* to be grumpy in the face of someone being happy, and *near impossible* to stay sullen rather than succumb to the joyous attitude of a happy person in your midst. Major Burns had little choice, for that young lady's happy and positive manner was simply too infectious to be ignored and too powerful to be deflected.

Surely we all know just being around a happy person can't change our mood from sour to sweet, but it can make it much harder for us to sustain that bad mood. It's clearly naïve to believe that simply being nice to people who disagree with us can convince them to change their minds but it may at least make them hear us out. Without a doubt it's way too simplistic to think being nice to people who are angry with us will turn them into our best friends, but it could disarm them enough to allow us to mend fences or soothe wounds. Quite simply, it's difficult not to get caught up in a wave of kindness and likeability when it's right in front of you. Just as that young woman on *M*A*S*H* changed the behavior and character of her would-be detractor, and that cab driver changed my mean-spirited mood on that way-too-early morning, as teachers we can just as surely help change the attitude of a surly student, ingratiate ourselves to parents and administrators, or lift the disposition of an entire class of young people simply with our attitudes.

I know this approach may seem a bit manipulative, but it works, and it does so in a most positive and uplifting way. I know there will be times that being nice to someone we are angry with will be difficult but this just may be the best course of action. I know there will be days when we just aren't in the mood to be nice; what then? Well strangely enough, on those days we are a bit grumpy but still can muster the wherewithal to pull this off, guess whose mood is the first to turn upward? Our own. Guess who is the first beneficiary of a better disposition? We are. Because it's hard to be grouchy around someone who isn't, even if that some-one is us!

Is this always the best approach? No. Will it always work perfectly? No. But can being a positive force, helping lift people's moods with your very spirit, or being perceived as nice, be a bad thing? I figure it's like the wonderful joke about the physician who prescribes chicken soup to an old man suffering from the common cold. After hearing this recommendation the patient asks, "Are you sure this will help?" To which the doctor replies, "No, but it couldn't hurt!" So the next time you're confronted with surly, be cheerful, because it's nice to be nice to the nice. Try it; what do you have to lose?

I guess it all comes down to one simple thought and a very profound question: "Attitudes are contagious. Are yours worth catching?" ▨

CREATIVITY

One morning many years ago, one of my children, sitting at the kitchen table looking very sleepy as he tried to wake up during breakfast before heading off to school, asked me, "Why do we have to go to school?" Surely every parent has heard that question, and just as surely you can bet I gave the perfunctory answer "Because," followed quickly with a diatribe about the virtues of learning as much as one can. But it got me thinking. Why *do* children need to go to school?

Of course we want them to learn information, gain skills, develop the ability to function as productive members of society, learn to communicate, think and feel. But of all that we can instill in our students, I believe creativity would have to be toward the top of the list. Being armed with information is important, but couple that with creativity and you can change a life. Possessing many skills is wonderful, but link those skills with creativity and you can change a community. Being able to communicate is vital, but combine that with creativity and you can change the world.

But what makes someone creative? Why do some people seem to be more creative than others? Is it remarkable intelligence or profound knowledge so that only the smartest among us are destined to be the creative thinkers? Strangely, no. Conversely, often some of the most creative people on earth are of average intelligence. So if it's not intelligence, what makes someone creative? More important, how can we instill, teach and foster creative thinking in our classrooms? How can we help encourage the creative seed that rests inside all of us?

Though I have taken part in more than my fair share of group sessions designed to develop creativity through various exercises—and don't get me wrong, they were quite a lot of fun—they always left me invigorated to be creative, but unable to know how. How *does* someone act creatively? What do creative people do differently than noncreative people? What can I do to be more creative aside from simply trying to be so?

Then one day I found the answers I had been looking for in the pages of a wonderful book entitled *Cracking Creativity*. "Typically," writes author Michael Michalko, "we think reproductively, on the basis of similar problems encountered in the past. When confronted with problems, we fixate on something in our past that has worked before. We ask, 'What have I been taught in my life, education, or work that will solve this problem?' Then we analytically select the most promising approach based on past experiences, excluding all other approaches, and work in a clearly defined direction toward the solution of the problem. Because of the apparent soundness of the steps based on past experiences, we become arrogantly certain of the correctness of our conclusion."

After reading that passage for the first time, I thought, "So what's wrong with that?" That's what keeps us from putting our fingers in a light socket or touching a hot stove. That's how we know how to balance a checkbook or do a purchase order (well maybe not a purchase order, since I will go to my grave not understanding that mystery!). How could knowing what worked in the past so we can do it again be a bad thing?

Do you know what the problem with reproductive thinking is? It works! That's right, it works and because it works so well and is so ingrained in us, we use it all the time. Because of that, Michalko cautions, "Once we have an idea we think works, it becomes hard for us to consider alternative ideas." "Reproductive thinking leads us to the usual ideas and not to original ones."

In contrast, he goes on to say, creative geniuses think *productively*, revealing that, "when confronted with a problem, they ask themselves how many different ways they can look at the problem, how they can rethink it, and how many different ways they can solve it, instead of asking how they have been taught to solve it. They tend to come up with many different responses, some of which are unconventional, and possibly, unique." He continues, "With productive thinking, one generates as many alternative approaches as one can, considering the least as well as the most likely approaches. It is the willingness to explore all approaches that is important, even after one has found a promising one."

Basically, less creative people will stop looking for ideas once they think of a "good" one, whereas highly creative people continue to come up with ideas long after finding a good one, in the hopes of finding a great one. In short, we can never let the *good idea* become the enemy of finding the *great idea*.

In an amazingly illuminating example, Michalko writes that "Einstein was once asked what the difference was between him and the average person. He said that if you asked the average person to find a needle in a haystack, the person would stop when he or she found a needle. He, on the other hand, would tear through the entire haystack looking for all the possible needles."

To this end, creative individuals seem to use their imaginations less encumbered by strictures, patterns of thought, boundaries and entrenched notions. They are somehow better able to suspend associations from past experiences and remove predictability and logic from their thought process, thus allowing them to think of many more ideas as well as wildly innovative and unusual possibilities. Along the way they question every aspect of what they "know to be true." In fact, as creative individuals, we are sometimes better served by great questions than by great answers.

Sadly, during the process of generating ideas, less creative individuals seem to be far more tempered by stereotypes, labels or past associations, often so focused on what they consciously or subconsciously believe to be obvious facts they miss the hidden features, essential relationships or counterintuitive functions just off the beaten path.

For example, if I were to ask you to invent a sandwich, would your past associations limit your imagination to starting with two slices of white bread or would you have been creative enough to think of pulling out a loaf of raisin bread? Would you have been inventive enough to begin with two slices of French toast? Maybe, but would old associations have kept you starting your recipe with "take one slice of bread" even if you did test the creative waters of what kind of bread? Or would you have come up with a delicious recipe that uses breaded fried green tomato slices as the outside of the "sandwich," or two leaves of lettuce, or two sheets of edible paper?

To explain, Michalko poses a wonderful question: "Suppose you were given a candle, a corkboard, and a box of tacks. Can you fasten the candle in such a way that it does not drip on the floor?" Think about it. What did you come up with? Typically, he states, "...most people have great difficulty coming up with a solution. However, when people are given a candle, corkboard, and the thumbtacks and the box separately, most solve the problem quickly. In the first case, the box containing the tacks is subject to a particular association. Participants see it only as a container for tacks, not as a possible wall fixture for the candle. When it is separated out, participants quickly are able to see how they could use it to solve the problem by tacking the box to the wall as a platform and placing the candle on top. (The function of any object is not inherent in the object itself but develops from our observation and association with it.)"

As one final example, this wonderful story by Bruce Vaughn illustrates how first "solutions" or "answers" can be as expedient as they are wrong. "There are two barbers in a small, isolated town. One barber's shop is littered with hair all over the floor. His own hair is a mess and he appears to be disorganized. The other barber's shop is clean and well organized. His hair is neat and looks nice. Which barber do you go to for a haircut?

"Working only from the information given above, you'd be wise to go to the unkempt barber with the messy shop. Being that the town is small and isolated, one can safely assume he gets his hair cut by the barber with the clean shop, whose shop is probably so organized because he doesn't get much business. Not to mention, his hair is neat and looks nice — probably the handiwork of the only other barber in town — the messy one."

It seems by simply thinking of what we see and hear — the *content* we perceive — in many and different *contexts*, we expand our creative palate. Looking at the same old event or information in varied and atypical ways can change its meaning, give new perspectives and become a catalyst for creative ideas.

It all comes down to this: if our knee-jerk response is always to do what worked before, how can we possibly ever come up with a better way? If we assume certain ways to be the best or only way of doing something or solving a problem, then every decision we make will be tainted by that assumption. In that way, as Stephen R. Covey so simply cautioned, often "the way we see the problem is the problem."

This way of thinking about creativity goes well beyond simple brainstorming or "thinking outside the box." True creativity, it seems, comes from forcing ourselves not to be prejudiced by our past successes as well as our failures. It demands a willingness and desire to think of many answers to a problem and worry about their validity or usefulness later. It warrants the perspective that sometimes large solutions may be the result of many little creative steps rather than just one big imaginative answer. Thus realizing, as Bill Willcox wrote, "The only thing standing between one big creative idea and success is about a million small creative solutions."

Even if some of those ideas didn't work once before or were deemed impractical in the past, they may end up being useful now. "For example," as Jack Gillett and Gary Schnuckle quipped, "the wheel existed for a long time in millstones before man used it for transportation. Why was that? There were no roads. But, inevitably, nice flat surfaces were invented, leading to wheeled vehicles. If your idea is way out, keep going, keep pushing. In doing so, perhaps you'll invent roads for your wheels." Or as James Russell Lowell put it, "Creativity is not the finding of a thing, but the making something out of it when it is found."

So I guess when we are filling out those purchase orders, the "same old way that worked before" may be the best bet, but when we are trying to set free our creative spirits, let us resolve not to grab the old familiar answers but reveal as many as we can, finding all those needles in all those haystacks. More important, let's resolve to help our students learn to do the same.

"It is always about discovering what, hidden, does not lie on the paper," affirmed the legendary musician Andres Segovia. As teachers what could be more important than teaching our students that truth, about music and so much of life, by helping them discover the creative spark in each of them? In so doing, we gently place in the hands of all those whom we teach the ability and responsibility for the power of music, that wonder and beauty expressed through creative minds, hearts and souls. █

THE SPIRIT OF
THE GIFT

I n his wonderful book, *All I Really Need to Know I Learned in Kindergarten*, Robert Fulghum tells the story of V. P. Menon, a man of humble beginnings who rose to become a significant political figure during India's struggle for independence from Britain. Menon, the eldest of twelve children, quit school at thirteen to work as a laborer before taking a job as a government clerk. Rising to the highest ranks, he was eventually praised by both Nehru and Lord Mountbatten for his important role in helping to bring freedom to his homeland. He was also known for his charity, explained by Fulghum with the following story.

"When Menon arrived in Delhi to seek a job in government, all his possessions, including his money and I.D., were stolen at the railroad station. He would have to return home on foot, defeated. In desperation he turned to an elderly Sikh, explaining his troubles, and asking for a temporary loan of fifteen rupees to tide him over until he could get a job. The Sikh gave him the money. When Menon asked for his address so that he could repay the man, the

Sikh said that Menon owed the debt to any stranger who came to him in need, as long as he lived. The help came from a stranger and was to be repaid to a stranger.

"Menon never forgot that debt. Neither the gift of trust nor the fifteen rupees. His daughter said that the day before Menon died, a beggar came to the family home in Bangalore asking for help to buy new sandals, for his feet were covered with sores. Menon asked his daughter to take fifteen rupees out of his wallet to give to the man. It was Menon's last conscious act.

"This story was told to me by a man whose name I do not know. He was standing beside me in the Bombay airport at the left-baggage counter. I had come to reclaim my bags and had no Indian currency left. The agent would not take a traveler's check, and I was uncertain about getting my luggage and making my plane. The man paid my claim-check fee—about eighty cents—and told me the story as a way of refusing my attempts to figure out how to repay him. His father had been Menon's assistant and had learned Menon's charitable ways and passed them on to his son. The son had continued the tradition of seeing himself in debt to strangers, whenever, however."

Fulghum goes on to write, "The gift was not large as money goes, and my need was not great, but the spirit of the gift is beyond price and leaves me blessed and in debt."

In so many ways I think this story describes education. Every moment we teach aren't we continuing a similar cycle? Our teachers helped us learn, not so we may repay that knowledge back to them, but so we can pass it on to others, who in turn may pass it on to still others.

As well, every time we empower children to stand on their own, dream of more than they thought possible, cherish their world or delight in their potential aren't we in fact helping them to share *those* very gifts with others, who will continue to share them? Those gifts may indeed not be great but they are truly priceless and timeless.

As that wise old Sikh passed his gift to Menon, who passed it on to his assistant, who passed it on to his son, who passed it on to Robert Fulghum, who passed it on to me, who passed it on to you so that you can pass it on to others, so go the music lessons, and more important, the life lessons our students learn from us.

Will any one deed change the world? Can any small event change a life? Who knows. But surely all we do will travel far beyond the walls of our schools through the minds, hearts and souls of our students. It is a profound responsibility but also an amazing opportunity. We must cherish that notion, guard it, honor it and savor it. For long after we are gone the essence of who we were and what we did, the spirit of those gifts, will forever be carried on by those we have taught.

I guess it all boils down to the simple power of the words of Bruce Barton: "Sometimes when I consider what tremendous consequences come from little things . . . I am tempted to think . . . here are no little things."

"PERCHÉ?"

F unny thing about wisdom, you never know where you'll
find it. Sometimes it's found in the pages of a book.
Sometimes it's found in the words of a scholar. Sometimes it
comes from great teachers. Sometimes it comes from great
philosophers. But sometimes it is in the face of a three-year-
old child. And how gloriously profound that can be. One
such time I will never forget.

I left my hotel room early one morning, stopped by a
corner café for a cup of espresso or three, then set out walking around town. As I strolled through this beautiful city I
saw gorgeous architecture, stunning facades and breathtaking views interrupted only briefly by the occasional passing
fireboat, ambulance boat, police boat, mail boat and *UPS*
delivery boat. It was after a few of those I said to myself,
"Peter, you're not in Kansas anymore." I wasn't; it was Venice, Italy.

Venice, one of the most amazing places on earth, with
its winding maze of canals, is a marvel of ingenuity and
resourcefulness. In that my hotel was on one side of town,
I decided to spend the day walking across the city seeing
as much as I could, meandering from site to site. By late

afternoon, there I was on the other side of this celebrated city, standing in the Piazza San Marco staring in awe at the power and grace of the grand Basilica di San Marco. By day's end, I was exhilarated and invigorated. I was also exhausted.

At that point I decided not to walk back to my hotel, but rather to jump on a water bus. Just like any bus running through any city, it's just that this flotilla of floating public transportation stops at various places as it circumnavigates the Grand Canal. So I wandered over to the stop conveniently located right at the Piazza, checked my map and figured out that I needed the number 82 water bus bound for San Marcuola, the closest stop to my hotel. After only a few moments one pulled up to the dock-stop and I hopped on.

I took my seat on a bench at the front of the boat, right along the railing, in the open air where I planned on taking in as much of the view as possible. Off we went, floating along this beautiful waterway moving from stop to stop. I was captivated by each building, each picturesque scene and the gentle wake of each passing boat. I was truly mesmerized. Then in the distance I saw my stop. San Marcuola now in sight, I moved to the disembarking area of the boat. There I stood and watched as we floated right *past* my stop. Puzzled, I re-checked my map. Sure enough, I *was* right, I *did* need the number 82 boat. Unfortunately, I soon realized, I must not be on one. So I stuck my head over the side and sure enough, there was the placard clearly stating this was a number 4 water bus.

After another check of my map, it seemed the best solution was to take a seat and enjoy the ride all the way around the *entire* city. So I did. I made my way back to my bench seat and sat down for the ride. Though this time, right along the rail next to me sat a beautiful little girl with eyes the size of the sun, though twice as brilliant. On either side of her were her grandfather and grandmother, each with a face wreathed with expressions of love and warmth.

As we traveled along the canal I couldn't help but watch this trio as much as the view around me. At one point I heard the grandfather speak to the little girl as he pointed out something in the water. But since my Italian is even worse than my water bus choosing, I couldn't understand a single word. Then the little girl looked at him and said, "Perché?" And even though I can't tell a 4 from an 82, I did know her response was a simple "why?"

To that her grandfather rattled off a lengthy answer, only to be followed with another "perché." Unwavering, he eloquently came back with a lengthy explanation which again was followed by another "perché" from this precious child. This went on for quite some time, the grandfather showing the patience of a saint, the child showing the curiosity of an inventor. I was fascinated by each passing answer and each questioning "why." Over and over, back and forth they went. She wanted to know why and no answer seemed to suffice. I don't know how many times I heard her mantra of "perché," but it went on for some time as we shared this ride around the city of Venice.

After quite a long while, the little girl and her slightly worn-out grandparents came to their stop. As they moved toward the exit, the grandfather nodded to me and waved. "Your granddaughter is charming and delightful," I said to the kindly old man as he smiled with pride. I knew I would never see them again, but I was so glad I took the wrong water bus and providence allowed me to spend some time with them.

Even though I could understand only one word of the lengthy conversation, it reminded me of one of the only things that really matters in teaching: getting a child to ask "why." Not just ask it, but dwell on it, ponder it, stew over it, insist upon it, dream about it and savor it. One little word that can lead a child to discover anything, learn anything and become anything. One word — one simple word — that can change a child's life. I dare say that little or nothing we teach may be as important as never letting a child lose that curiosity, that desire to ask "why." For doesn't everything else flow from that?

Now, I have three children. I have obviously heard my share of "why." So what made that event, that day, on that water bus crystallize into such a powerful experience? What brought it so vividly to mind? I don't know. Maybe it was the magnificence of the surroundings, maybe it was the fact that I understood nothing but that one word, maybe it was because the faces of those people were so captivating, maybe it was because that precious three-year-old child had such powerful intensity, but maybe it was the fact that I only knew the question, not the answer.

I will never forget that city. I will never forget that day. I will never forget that child. But most important, I hope to never forget the power of helping young people cherish the joy of asking "why." If we can simply get students to ask, with just that one word, the mind wanders, the senses percolate, the memory searches and the heart yearns. In short, they will learn to spend their life finding the answers, because they will have all the right questions.

I know I will never see that charming little girl again but I have no worries about her. I have no doubt she will become nothing less than what she sets her mind to become. Because she surely knows how to look at her world, find the eyes of a loving grandfather and simply ask — no, demand — to know "why."

BREAK A LEG

Have you ever thought about that phrase? I mean ever *really* thought about it. We use it all the time, bantering it around to our colleagues and students as a frothy way of wishing them luck before a performance. You've probably had it said to you as often as you've said it to others as a sarcastic quip of humorous irony and incongruous wit. However to me those words are anything but silly, anything but amusing. In fact the power of that phrase grounds me with its importance, excites me with its promise and reminds me of the solemn responsibility of our work every time I hear it.

Though there are many explanations for how that odd trio of words can be explained and has found its way into common usage, the one I choose to believe comes from the days of Victorian theater. A time that "proper" was the order of the day and formality was as important as correctness. Legend has it that as actors or actresses took the stage, those three words would be said to them by their fellow performers to encourage them to have a remarkable performance. Not as a cute, superstitious, tongue-in-cheek "slap on the back," but as a profoundly serious hope.

For you see, back then, if an actor's performance was very good and met with the audience's approval he was permitted to come to the edge of the stage and bow with a sincere nodding of the head as the rest of his body stayed straight and tall. If the performance was so appreciated as to receive great applause he was allowed to bow by bending forward from the waist. But if the actor's work was so special, so fantastic, so extraordinary as to have the audience respond with a rousing ovation, then the actor could come to the edge of that stage and bow by putting one foot out in front of him as he almost bent down on one knee, so as to truly *break a leg*.

To me this simple phrase is a reminder of how important we are in the lives of our students, how we must cherish every opportunity to nurture them, how great a responsibility education is and how each moment of our teaching must be the best we can muster. It reminds me that the promise we make as teachers is profound, the promise each new day holds is limitless and the promise each student possesses is infinite. It helps me remember the joys of teaching, those gifts which are as intangible as they are amazing. For whatever the name we call teacher, and there are many, the rewards may be as subtle as an unspoken word, as simple as a tentative smile or as profound as a tender tear.

It brings focus to the goal of our own planned obsolescence, teaching students as much about *how* to learn and *why* the joy of learning is as exciting as the subject matter itself. It reassures me that the greatest gift we can give our students is the knowledge they can move beyond our time with them, confident they no longer need us. For we surely know that the real gifts we receive are ultimately those we give. As Pericles so eloquently put it, "What you leave behind is not what is engraved in stone monuments, but what is woven into the lives of others." Or in the words of St. Francis: "Remember that when you leave this earth, you can take nothing you have received...but only what you have given...."

As teachers we can do no better than to remember, "We never know how far-reaching something we may think, say, or do today will affect the life of a child tomorrow." Those *tomorrows* that we plant today for every child, confident in the wisdom of Robert Lewis Stevenson who cautioned, "Don't judge each day by the harvest you reap, but by the seeds you plant." Those *seeds* that will always be a part of each student we touch, or as Rodger Austin so perfectly stated, "Sometimes people, who come into your life, make changes in you...because you always take a little part of them with you into the future. We are all made up of little bits and pieces of those whose lives touch ours."

Reflect for a moment on those amazing teachers in your life and the little bits and pieces of them you took with you, that you keep with you, that you cherish, that help make you who you are today. Those are the little bits and pieces which every one of your students will take with them: a spoken word or simple deed, an igniting thought or knowing smile.

No words express this better than those which follow. They have been attributed to many and though we may never truly come to know their author, the power of the sentiment crystallizes who we are and what we do as teachers: "Watch your thoughts, for they become words. Watch your words, for they become actions. Watch your actions, for they become habits. Watch your habits, for they become character. Watch your character, for it becomes your destiny." Far more important, as teachers our thoughts, words, actions and habits will help shape the character and destiny of every child we touch. That, my friends, is *our* destiny, is *our* legacy, is what John Allston meant when he counseled, "The only thing you take with you when you're gone is what you leave behind."

We all know teachers rarely leave behind massive fortunes that can be counted or tremendous monuments that can be filmed. But in so many ways they are quiet heroes in the lives of their students. Heroes that make a difference in ways that are intangible, invisible and unknowable but are nonetheless as rich as any fortune, as grand as any monument. I guess our destiny as teachers can best be explained in the words of the popular video game *Halo 3* which affirms, "A hero need not speak. When he is gone, the world will speak for him." As teachers much of our world is our students and they indeed will speak for us, now and long after we are gone.

So with all this and much more at stake, it is clear our work is much more than a career, it's a calling. A calling we were drawn to by the promise of the joy it holds for us, our students and all of humanity. Who knows whether music chose us for this calling or we chose music, but either way, let us hope that each of us may work to teach so well as to earn the title of teacher, to finish each of our days, each of our years and ultimately each of our careers confident we deserve to *break a leg*.

"I Always Thought I
Had Tomorrow"

"Dear Peter, I'm writing to you because I thought you could help. But I know you can't. No one can." So the letter began from a music teacher friend of mine. "Yesterday was just a normal day around here. I started with a few rehearsals, then a couple of lessons, my normal lunch and hall duty, ending with a rehearsal last period. It wasn't the best day of my teaching career, but it wasn't the worst day either. It was just a normal average day. After school, I taught a couple of make-up lessons, did a little paperwork, made a few phone calls and headed off for home. It was just normal. It was just average.

"Then I heard the news. On her way home from school, a student, one of my students, was in a car accident. She died at the scene. Word went around our small town like wildfire. It hit me like a ton of bricks. This wasn't some nameless, faceless person I saw on the front page of a newspaper; it was one of my students. She wasn't the best alto sax player I ever had but she was one of mine.

"I keep trying to remember back to that last period rehearsal we had together, wondering if I made it matter. I just don't know. I know I didn't holler at her, or say anything mean to her. But I don't remember much of anything else either, because it was just a normal average day.

"Now, everything I thought I knew is different. My life changed yesterday. Nothing seems the same. Nothing will be normal again. I wish I had told her how proud I was of her, that she was doing better and that I appreciated her effort. I wish I had made her smile or given her that pat on the back. But I didn't, and now I can't.

"I know there is nothing I can do now, and there is nothing you can say, but I just needed to share this with someone. I wish I had done any of those things. When I think about it, I guess I didn't because I always thought I had tomorrow. But for her, I never had tomorrow."

There have been very few times in my life that I have been rendered speechless. Reading that letter was one of them. I didn't know what to say. I didn't know what to do. I sat and looked at a blank computer screen with tears streaming down my face, not having any idea what to write. He was correct: there was nothing I could say. No words could console him, no words could help him, no words could make it better.

As I sat there helpless, thoughts of my own students filled my head. How often they must leave my class or rehearsal not knowing how much they matter. How often I assume that with enough tomorrows I'll get to making them all feel special. Sadly there aren't always those tomorrows.

Over the weeks that followed that day, I thought — ever more profoundly — about the time I had with my students and how very precious it was. I became more conscious of every moment. In rehearsals I often found myself looking at a student thinking, "What if these are the last words we share?" What would I say? What would I find myself someday wishing I would have said? Though I had never thought about it before, I guess I too always thought I had tomorrow. I always thought I had more time. But as Anna Nalick reminds us, "Life's like an hourglass glued to the table." And not only can't we stop those sands of time, or turn that hourglass over, we don't even know how long that hourglass lasts.

Time: that most precious of commodities. The time we have our students in rehearsals. The time we have our students in our sphere of influence. The time we have to do meaningful things for our students. The time we have to share the joy of making music with them. The time we have to make it matter, to make no day in life a "normal average" day. The time to teach our students to value, savor and cherish every passing moment.

My friend was right in so many ways. I couldn't help him. But *he* helped *me*. This tragedy reminded me that no day can be average or normal. Each must be special and treasured, *just like our students.*

I used to believe I had plenty of tomorrows with my students. Since that day my greatest fear as a teacher is that I won't. I find myself asking whether I would say, do or be anything different if I knew today would be the last time I would see one of my students ever again.

It is said that time is our worst enemy. That may be true, but regret can't be far behind, and for a teacher what greater regret could there be than to be faced with the realization that there will be no more tomorrows for a child?

So now when I look into the eyes of my students I'm much more careful, much more worried. But I also find more joy, enjoy more smiles and delight more fully in the time I share with them, trying all the while to count that time by the moments that matter rather than the minutes that simply pass. Heaven knows I pray the day will never come when I would have to say the last sentence of his letter—"But for her, I never had tomorrow"—but if I ever do, I hope I can find some comfort in the memories of the precious time we did get to share on this earth together.

I guess life really is that hourglass glued to a table. For tomorrow is a promise given to no one. No one. ▨

POSTLUDE:
PROMISES KEPT

I t never ceases to amaze me how special teachers are, made
up of equal parts guide, mentor, taskmaster, magician,
guardian, psychologist, cheerleader, optimist, inventor, artist, scholar, administrator, visionary and juggler. We share
many traits. We share many goals. Though we surely will dif-
fer on many aspects of education we are all bound by a love
of music, a love of working with young people and the joy
we feel from passing that art on to generations to come.

We are also bound by promises we make to our students
every day. Promises we each vow to honor when we take on
the noble responsibility we call teaching. No chapter can
list them all. No book can hold them. No words can truly
express them. Some of those promises may be as simple as a
caring smile, an expression of concern or an extra moment
of time. Other promises may be as profound as they are
daunting, as solemn as they are glorious.

Though in a teacher's life each moment can bring challenges, each day can bring concerns and each year brings
changes, a few promises rise high above that fray and are

at the very core of every teacher's being. Let each of us remember them, for they don't just help make a child's day, they can help make a child's life.

May we promise to teach them to love themselves. My great-grandmother lived to be ninety-six years of age, and though I was born after her passing, her advice for living a long and healthy life has been passed down through our family as an adage of sorts. She offered no long list of suggestions. As a matter of fact there was only one rule, and it had nothing to do with eating well, exercising, meditating or medicine. It was simply to "never envy anyone." With each passing day of my life the wisdom of her words seems more profound and important.

Not just important for us as people but for us as teachers, as we help children learn to appreciate themselves, learn who they are, learn who they can become, learn what gifts they have and learn what gifts they are. To honor those words of my great-grandmother, what better goal could each of us have but to ensure that all of our students feel the only people they would want to be are *themselves?* For that is a promise worth keeping.

May we promise to teach them to love music. The remarkable Igor Stravinsky declared, "The trouble with music appreciation in general is that people are taught to have too much respect for music. They should be taught to love it instead." I marvel at his insight. Think about how often, even with the best of intentions, our efforts to help young people learn about something leads to them knowing a great deal about it, holding it in high esteem and understanding its significance, but often at the same time leaving them more intimidated by it than excited to embrace it.

Opera is a great example. You know opera, where, as Ed Gardner put it, "a guy gets stabbed in the back and, instead of bleeding, he sings." Seriously though, how many people were taught at a young age to understand opera when maybe they would have been better served to have been taught to love it instead? Surely true understanding and enjoyment go hand in hand, but that subtle balancing act may decide whether music is a subject learned or a passion ignited in our students.

While we're speaking of opera, as an aside having to do with nothing I must share my favorite opera story. It comes from the legendary Luciano Pavarotti, who offered up this opinion of what he had just heard: "Compare music to drinks: some is like a strong brandy. Some is like a fine wine. The music you're playing sounds like *Diet Coke*." (Sorry, I couldn't resist!)

Finally, may we promise to teach them to love life. It is said that the great Seneca cautioned, "Our care should not be to have lived long as to have lived enough." Though the older I get the more I hope for both, his words offer prudence to help guide every moment of our careers. The facts, skills and knowledge we teach are important in life but the creativity, expression and emotions we foster are important to living. Children knowing how to play a major scale is valuable; their having that ability to use as a tool to harness the creativity of their spirits and the warmth of their souls is priceless. That students know a date or place in music history is important; their having the ability to put themselves in that time or place through music is inestimable.

Leonardo da Vinci warned of what a terrible fate it would be for a person who "looks without seeing, listens without hearing, touches without feeling, eats without tasting, moves without physical awareness, inhales without awareness of odor or fragrance, and talks without thinking." Let us vow to help all of our students cherish what they see, marvel at what they hear, realize what they feel, savor what they taste, sense how they move, soak in every scent and speak with clarity of thought.

Through our teaching, through music, we can help children do just that, today, and for all of their tomorrows, helping to shape the destiny of all those whom we touch. Quite simply, "What sculpture is to a block of marble," Joseph Addison wrote, "education is to a human soul." Sometimes in the shuffle of all that needs to be done in our teaching day, the speed with which we must work, the grind of those daily frustrations which steal from our strength and the responsibility of the task at hand, it is easy to lose sight of the importance of those promises we make to our students, the joy of the promise of each new day and the promise that rests in the potential of every child.

Take the time to look into the eyes of your students and truly see who they are, who they can be, the triumphs of their successes, the tears of their failures, the emotions that come from the music they make, the power of their spirit and the splendor of their possibilities. Take time to realize every day how important you are in the lives of your students.

May the passion of what brought you to music empower you. May the purpose of what brought you to teaching swell your heart. May the promise of what brought you into the lives of all those whom you teach fill you with wonder, joy and happiness. ▪

ABOUT THE AUTHOR

Called "one of the most exciting and exhilarating voices in music education today," Peter Loel Boonshaft has been invited to speak or conduct in every state in the nation and around the world. He holds Bachelor of Music (Summa Cum Laude), Master of Music Education in Conducting, and Doctor of Musical Arts degrees. Dr. Boonshaft was also awarded a Connecticut General Fellowship for study at the Kodály Musical Training Institute, from which he holds a Certificate. He is currently on the faculty of Hofstra University in Hempstead, New York, where he is Professor of Music and Director of Bands. He is Conductor of the Hofstra University Wind Ensemble and Symphonic Band, professor of conducting and music education, and Director of the graduate wind conducting program. Prior to this appointment, Dr. Boonshaft was on the faculty of Moravian College and the University of Hartford. He was Founder and Music Director of the Pennsylvania Youth Honors Concert Band and the

Connecticut Valley Youth Wind Ensemble. In addition, he held the post of Music Director and Conductor of the Metropolitan Wind Symphony of Boston.

Dr. Boonshaft is the author of the critically acclaimed best selling books *Teaching Music with Passion* and *Teaching Music with Purpose*. He is also the author of *Vaclav Nelhybel: His Life and Works*, the only authorized biography of the composer; a contributing author of *The Music Director's Cookbook: Creative Recipes for a Successful Program;* and articles for *Instrumentalist Magazine*, the *National Band Association Journal*, MENC's *Teaching Music*, and *Band Director's Guide*. In addition, he holds the post of Band/Wind Ensemble Editor for the *School Music News*. Dr. Boonshaft has been a consultant or recorded for Boosey & Hawkes Music Publishers, Warner Brothers Publications, Southern Music Publishers, Kendor Music Publishers, Daehn Publications and C. Alan Music. Active as a proponent of new literature for concert band, he has commissioned and conducted over forty world premieres by such notable composers as Eric Ewazen, W. Francis McBeth, Johan de Meij, Fisher Tull, H. Owen Reed, Vaclav Nelhybel, David Gillingham, Philip Sparke, Sam Hazo, Andrew Boysen, Robert W. Smith, David Holsinger, Robert Washburn, Elliot Del Borgo, Herbert Deutsch, Ken Lampl, Robert Hawkins, Larry Lipkis, Ian McDougall, Rossano Galante, Reber Clark, Gregory Sanders, Roland Barrett and Jared Spears. Among the soloists who have appeared in performance with Dr. Boonshaft are John Marcellus, Maynard Ferguson, Harvey Phillips, Ed Shaughnessy, Lynn Klock, Don Butterfield, Dave Steinmeyer and the United States Air Force "Airmen of Note," Chester Schmitz, and the Vienna Schubert Trio.

Dr. Boonshaft has been awarded membership in Pi
Kappa Lambda and Alpha Chi, as well as twice receiving
the University of Hartford Regent's Award and that University's Outstanding Music Educator Award. He has received
official proclamations from the governors of four states and
a Certificate of Appreciation from former President Ronald
Reagan, as well as performing for former President and
Mrs. George Bush, former President Bill Clinton, and for
Margaret Thatcher, former prime minister of the United
Kingdom. His honors also include being selected three
times as a National Endowment for the Arts "Artist in Resi-
dence," three times awarded Honorary Life Membership in
the Tri-M Music Honor Society, and being selected for the
Center for Scholarly Research and Academic Excellence at
Hofstra University.

Extremely active as a guest conductor and speaker for
conferences, festivals, concerts and workshops nationally
and internationally, he has guest conducted the MENC
(The National Association for Music Education) All-East-
ern Band, MENC All-Northwest Band, MENC All-Eastern
Directors Band, and Goldman Memorial Band. He was also
named conductor of the MENC National High School
Honors Band. He has served as a speaker for the Canadian
Music Educators Association National Convention, MENC
National Conference, Midwest International Band and
Orchestra Clinic, Music For All/Bands and Orchestras of
America Symposium, Samuel Barber Institute for Music
Educators, Music Education Center of America, Conn-Sel-
mer Institute, NESA Council of Overseas Schools Confer-
ence in Bangkok, Thailand, and as keynote speaker for the
MENC Northwest Division Conference, MENC Southern

Division Conference, European Music Educators Convention, National Convention of the American String Teachers Association, National Convention of the American School Band Directors Association, ACDA Western Division Conference, and numerous state and regional music education conventions. ■

COMING SOON!

Teaching with

PASSION,
PURPOSE,
and
PROMISE

 PETER LOEL BOONSHAFT

**For Teachers of All Academic Subjects
(Math, Science, History, etc.)**